THE AUSTRALIAN
Women's Weekly
superfast recipes

acp
books

Contents

on the table in 10 minutes

cheesy ham omelette

8 eggs, separated
¼ cup finely chopped fresh chives
⅓ cup (25g) finely grated parmesan cheese
30g (1 ounce) butter
125g (4 ounces) smoked ham, chopped finely
⅔ cup (80g) coarsely grated gruyère cheese

1 Beat egg whites in large bowl with electric mixer until soft peaks form. Combine egg yolks, half the chives and parmesan in large bowl. Gently fold whites into yolk mixture.
2 Heat one-quarter of the butter in a small frying pan; add one-quarter of the egg mixture, sprinkle with one-quarter of the combined ham and gruyère. Cook over medium heat until mixture is almost set. Fold omelette in half, transfer to plate; sprinkle with some of the remaining chives. Cover to keep warm.
3 Repeat step 2 to make a further 3 omelettes.

prep + cook time 10 minutes **serves** 4
nutritional count per serving 25.8g total fat
(12.8g saturated fat); 1425kJ (341 cal);
0.5g carbohydrate; 27.3g protein; 0.1g fibre

serving suggestion Tomato salsa or chutney and crusty bread.

note Gruyère cheese is a swiss cheese having small holes and a nutty, slightly salty, flavour.

steak sandwiches

4 beef scotch fillet steaks (600g)
¼ cup (75g) dijonnaise
8 thick slices ciabatta bread, toasted
50g mixed salad leaves
2 medium tomatoes (300g), sliced thickly
⅓ cup (110g) capsicum relish

1 Season steaks well on both sides. Cook steaks on heated oiled barbecue (or grill or grill pan).
2 Spread dijonnaise on toasted bread slices. Sandwich salad leaves, steaks, tomato and relish between toast slices.

prep + cook time 10 minutes **serves** 4
nutritional count per serving 15.9g total fat (4.7g saturated fat); 2646kJ (633 cal); 72.1g carbohydrate; 45.4g protein; 8.4g fibre

notes Dijonnaise is a blend of mayonnaise and dijon mustard; plain mayonnaise can be used instead, or spread sandwiches with your favourite chutney, relish or sauce.
Try sourdough bread instead of the ciabatta.

veal steaks with caper lemon butter sauce

1 tablespoon cracked black pepper
6 thin veal schnitzels (600g), halved (see note)
60g (2 ounces) butter
1 tablespoon rinsed, drained baby capers
3 strips lemon rind, sliced thinly
⅓ cup (80ml) lemon juice
⅓ cup coarsely chopped fresh flat-leaf parsley

1 Sprinkle pepper on both sides of steaks. Heat butter in large frying pan; cook steaks, in batches, until browned lightly both sides. Transfer steaks to serving plates.
2 Add capers, rind, juice and 1 tablespoon water to pan; bring to the boil, stirring. Spoon sauce over steaks; sprinkle with parsley.

prep + cook time 10 minutes **serves** 4
nutritional count per serving 14.6g total fat
(8.7g saturated fat); 1137kJ (272 cal);
1.1g carbohydrate; 33.8g protein; 0.4g fibre

note Veal schnitzel is thinly sliced steak available crumbed or plain (uncrumbed); we used plain schnitzel, also called escalopes, in this recipe.

spinach, chorizo and roast capsicum salad

2 chorizo sausages (340g), sliced thinly
125g (4 ounces) baby spinach leaves
310g (10 ounces) canned chickpeas (garbanzo), rinsed, drained
125g (4 ounces) char-grilled red capsicum, sliced thinly
1 tablespoon red wine vinegar

1 Cook chorizo in heated large frying pan until browned both sides. Drain on absorbent paper. Add spinach to same pan; cook, uncovered, until spinach is wilted.
2 Place spinach, chickpeas, capsicum, vinegar and chorizo in large bowl; toss gently.

prep + cook time 10 minutes **serves** 4
nutritional count per serving 27.6g total fat (9.6g saturated fat); 1597kJ (382 cal); 11g carbohydrate; 21.1g protein; 4.1g fibre

note Char-grilled capsicum is available, in slices, from delicatessens, or bottled, in oil or brine, from many supermarkets.

tomato, mozzarella and prosciutto salad

3 slices prosciutto (45g)
3 large egg (plum) tomatoes (270g),
  chopped coarsely
300g (9½ ounces) cherry bocconcini cheese,
  chopped coarsely
1 medium avocado (250g), chopped coarsely
125g (4 ounces) mixed salad leaves
2 tablespoons olive oil

1 Cook prosciutto in heated medium frying pan until crisp; drain on absorbent paper. When cool enough to handle, break into pieces.
2 Combine prosciutto, tomato, cheese, avocado and salad leaves in serving bowl. Drizzle with oil; season to taste.

prep + cook time 10 minutes **serves** 4
nutritional count per serving 31.2g total fat (11.2g saturated fat); 1488kJ (356 cal); 1.8g carbohydrate; 16.9g protein; 2.1g fibre

prawn and pesto linguine

375g (12 ounces) linguine pasta
500g (1 pound) shelled uncooked large
  green prawns (shrimp)
2 cloves garlic, crushed
1 fresh long red chilli, sliced thinly
1 medium zucchini (120g), cut into ribbons
180g (6 ounces) bottled chunky basil pesto dip

1 Cook pasta in large saucepan of boiling water until tender; drain, reserving ⅓ cup cooking liquid. Return pasta to pan.
2 Meanwhile, heat oiled large frying pan; cook prawns until changed in colour. Add garlic, chilli and zucchini to pan; cook, uncovered, until zucchini softens.
3 Add pesto, prawn mixture and reserved cooking liquid to pasta; toss gently.

prep + cook time 10 minutes **serves** 4
nutritional count per serving 19.8g total fat (4.2g saturated fat); 2571kJ (615 cal); 65.1g carbohydrate; 40.9g protein; 4.9g fibre

note Use a vegetable peeler to cut the succhini into ribbons.

antipasto vegetable salad with minted yogurt

¼ cup coarsely chopped fresh mint
1 clove garlic, crushed
¾ cup (200g) greek-style yogurt
270g (9 ounces) bottled char-grilled antipasto,
  drained, chopped coarsely
310g (10 ounces) canned chickpeas (garbanzo),
  rinsed, drained
100g (3 ounces) mixed salad leaves

1 Combine mint, garlic and yogurt in small bowl.
2 Combine antipasto, chickpeas and salad leaves
in large bowl; toss gently.
3 Serve salad drizzled with minted yogurt.

prep time 10 minutes **serves** 4
nutritional count per serving 4.2g total fat
(1.5g saturated fat); 631kJ (151 cal);
16.4g carbohydrate; 8.5g protein; 6.4g fibre

warm balsamic mushroom salad

8 slices pancetta (120g)
½ cup (125ml) balsamic italian dressing
500g (1 pound) small button mushrooms
1 teaspoon fresh thyme leaves
90g (3 ounces) mixed salad leaves
90g (3 ounces) fetta cheese, crumbled

1 Cook pancetta in heated oiled large frying pan until crisp. When cool enough to handle, break into large pieces.
2 Heat dressing and ⅓ cup water in same frying pan; cook mushrooms and thyme, stirring, until mushrooms are tender and liquid has almost evaporated. Season to taste.
3 Combine mushrooms, salad leaves and pancetta in large bowl; toss gently. Serve topped with cheese.

prep + cook time 10 minutes **serves** 4
nutritional count per serving 19.9g total fat (6g saturated fat); 1066kJ (255 cal); 3.1g carbohydrate; 14.6g protein; 3.8g fibre

13

garlic and chilli mussels

60g (2 ounces) butter, chopped
3 cloves garlic, chopped finely
1 fresh long red chilli, sliced thinly
⅓ cup (80ml) dry white wine
1kg (2 pounds) small black mussels
⅓ cup coarsely chopped fresh flat-leaf parsley

1 Heat butter, garlic and chilli in large saucepan, stirring, until fragrant. Add wine; bring to the boil.
2 Add mussels to pan; simmer, covered, until mussels open (discard any that do not). Stir in parsley.

prep + cook time 10 minutes **serves** 4
nutritional count per serving 13.3g total fat (8.4g saturated fat); 702kJ (168 cal); 2.8g carbohydrate; 6.3g protein; 0.6g fibre

serving suggestion Crusty bread.

To save time, use pre-cleaned, bearded mussels.

piri piri fish with herb salad

4 firm white fish fillets (800g)
⅓ cup (80ml) piri piri marinade
80g baby rocket leaves (arugula)
⅓ cup firmly packed fresh mint leaves
¼ cup firmly packed fresh flat-leaf parsley leaves
1 tablespoon lemon juice

1 Drizzle fish with marinade, coating both sides.
Cook fish in heated oiled large frying pan.
2 Meanwhile, combine rocket, mint, parsley and
juice in medium bowl; season to taste.
3 Serve fish with salad.

prep + cook time 10 minutes **serves** 4
nutritional count per serving 5.1g total fat
(1.5g saturated fat); 991kJ (237 cal);
4.7g carbohydrate; 41.7g protein; 1.7g fibre

note We used blue eye in this recipe, but any
white fish fillet will be fine.

Piri piri, also spelled peri peri, is a hot chilli sauce used in African,
Portuguese and Brazilian cookery. It is available from gourmet
food stores and most major supermarkets.

smoky beans with chorizo

1 large red onion (300g), chopped coarsely

1 chorizo sausage (170g), chopped coarsely

1 large red capsicum (bell pepper) (350g),
  chopped coarsely

2 teaspoons smoked paprika

800g (28 ounces) canned borlotti beans,
  rinsed, drained

800g (28 ounces) canned crushed tomatoes

2 tablespoons coarsely chopped fresh
  flat-leaf parsley

1 Heat oiled large saucepan; cook onion, chorizo and capsicum, stirring, until vegetables are tender. Add paprika; cook, stirring, until fragrant.

2 Add beans and undrained tomatoes to pan; bring to the boil. Reduce heat; simmer, uncovered, about 5 minutes or until sauce is thickened.

3 Serve sprinkled with parsley.

prep + cook time 10 minutes **serves** 6
nutritional count per serving 9.4g total fat
(3.3g saturated fat); 1225kJ (293 cal);
33g carbohydrate; 15.9g protein; 6.2g fibre

serving suggestion Crusty bread.

pappardelle carbonara

375g (12 ounces) pappardelle pasta
8 slices prosciutto (60g), sliced thinly
3 eggs
½ cup (125ml) pouring cream
½ cup (40g) finely grated parmesan cheese
¼ cup coarsely chopped fresh flat-leaf parsley

1 Cook pasta in large saucepan of boiling water until just tender; drain, reserving ½ cup cooking liquid. Return pasta to pan over low heat.
2 Meanwhile, cook prosciutto in heated oiled large frying pan until crisp; remove from pan.
3 Combine eggs, cream and cheese in large jug. Add egg mixture, reserved pasta water, half the parsley and half the prosciutto to pasta; toss gently, season to taste.
4 Serve pasta topped with remaining parsley and prosciutto; season with pepper.

prep + cook time 10 minutes serves 4
nutritional count per serving 22.6g total fat
(12.7g saturated fat); 2349kJ (562 cal);
65g carbohydrate; 22.7g protein; 3.3g fibre

note Pappardelle is flat, wide pasta ribbons sometimes having scalloped edges. Tagliatelle or fettuccine can be substituted.

17

honey mustard lamb cutlets

1 tablespoon dijon mustard
1 tablespoon wholegrain (seeded) mustard
2 tablespoons honey
1 tablespoon white wine vinegar
12 french-trimmed lamb cutlets (600g)
400g (13 ounces) green beans, trimmed

1 Combine mustards, honey and vinegar in small jug. Combine half the honey mixture in large bowl; with cutlets.
2 Cook cutlets in heated oiled large frying pan.
3 Meanwhile, boil, steam or microwave beans until tender; drain.
4 Serve cutlets with green beans; drizzle with remaining honey mixture.

prep + cook time 10 minutes **serves** 4
nutritional count per serving 13.2g total fat (5.9g saturated fat); 1058kJ (253 cal); 4.5g carbohydrate; 17.7g protein; 2.9g fibre

grilled lamb chops with tomato and olive salsa

¼ cup loosely packed fresh oregano leaves
8 lamb loin chops (800g)
250g (8 ounces) cherry tomatoes, quartered
½ cup (75g) seeded kalamata olives, halved
2 tablespoons french dressing
100g (8 ounces) rocket (arugula)

1 Finely chop half the oregano; combine with chops in large bowl.
2 Season chops; cook on heated oiled grill pan (or grill or barbecue).
3 Meanwhile, to make tomato and olive salsa, combine tomato, olives, dressing and remaining oregano in medium bowl. Serve chops with salsa and rocket.

prep + cook time 10 minutes **serves** 4
nutritional count per serving 16.2g total fat (6.6g saturated fat); 1333kJ (319 cal); 8.2g carbohydrate; 33.9g protein; 2.2g fibre

grilled prawns with lemon grass and lime

60g (2 ounces) butter, softened
10cm (4 inch) stick fresh lemon grass (20g),
  chopped finely
2 teaspoons finely grated lime rind
2 tablespoons lime juice
2 tablespoons finely chopped fresh flat-leaf parsley
500g (1 pound) shelled uncooked medium
  king prawns (shrimp)

1 Beat butter, lemon grass, rind and juice in small bowl until combined; stir in parsley.
2 Melt half the butter mixture in large frying pan; remove from heat, stir in prawns.
3 Cook prawns on heated oiled barbecue (or grill or grill pan) until changed in colour. Serve prawns topped with remaining butter mixture.

prep + cook time 10 minutes **serves** 4
nutritional count per serving 13.1g total fat (8.2g saturated fat); 928kJ (222 cal); 0.3g carbohydrate; 25.9g protein; 0.2g fibre

serving suggestion Green salad and lime wedges.

teriyaki salmon

4 salmon fillets, skin on (880g)
2 tablespoons japanese soy sauce
2 tablespoons mirin seasoning
1 tablespoon light brown sugar
1 green onion (scallion), sliced thinly

1 Heat oiled large frying pan; cook salmon, skin-side down, about 5 minutes or until skin is crisp. Turn salmon; add sauce to pan with mirin, 2 tablespoons water and sugar; simmer, uncovered, until salmon is cooked as desired.
2 Serve salmon sprinkled with onion; drizzle over pan juices.

prep + cook time 10 minutes **serves** 4
nutritional count per serving 15.6g total fat
(3.5g saturated fat); 1404kJ (336 cal);
3.8g carbohydrate; 43.5g protein; 0.1g fibre

serving suggestion Steamed asian greens.

moroccan chicken with fruity couscous

12 chicken tenderloins (900g)
2 tablespoons moroccan seasoning
1¼ cups (250g) couscous
⅓ cup (55g) sultanas
⅓ cup (45g) slivered almonds, roasted
½ cup coarsely chopped fresh coriander (cilantro)
½ cup (140g) yogurt

1 Sprinkle chicken with seasoning; cook in heated oiled large frying pan.
2 Meanwhile, combine couscous with 1¼ cups boiling water in large heatproof bowl, cover; stand about 5 minutes or until water is absorbed, fluffing with fork occasionally. Stir in sultanas, nuts and coriander; season to taste.
3 Divide couscous into serving bowls; top with chicken and yogurt.

prep + cook time 10 minutes **serves** 4
nutritional count per serving 13g total fat (2.6g saturated fat); 2600kJ (622 cal); 60.4g carbohydrate; 63.3g protein; 2.5g fibre

creamy mushroom and spinach gnocchi

625g (1¼ pounds) fresh potato gnocchi
375g (12 ounces) assorted mushrooms, sliced thinly
2 cloves garlic, crushed
1¼ cups (310ml) pouring cream (see notes)
90g (3 ounces) baby spinach leaves
⅓ cup (25g) finely grated parmesan cheese

1 Cook gnocchi in large saucepan of boiling water until tender; drain.
2 Meanwhile, cook mushrooms and garlic in heated oiled large frying pan, stirring, until softened. Add cream and spinach; bring to the boil. Reduce heat, simmer, uncovered, until spinach wilts and sauce thickens. Stir in half the cheese. Season to taste.
3 Add gnocchi to pan, stir gently. Serve gnocchi topped with remaining cheese.

prep + cook time 10 minutes **serves** 4
nutritional count per serving 36.2g total fat (23.4g saturated fat); 2458kJ (588 cal); 48.2g carbohydrate; 14.4g protein; 6.8g fibre

notes It is fine to use just 1 x 300ml carton of cream for this recipe.
Try using a variety of mushrooms such as flat, cup, button and portobello.

garlicky lemon chicken

Cook 6 halved chicken thigh fillets in heated oiled large frying pan. Add 2 tablespoons coarsely chopped fresh flat-leaf parsley, 3 crushed garlic cloves, 2 teaspoons finely grated lemon rind, 2 tablespoons lemon juice and 1 tablespoon water to pan. Turn chicken to coat; season to taste.

prep + cook time 10 minutes **serves** 4
nutritional count per serving 21.7g total fat (6.6g saturated fat); 1760kJ (421 cal); 0.6g carbohydrate; 56.1g protein; 0.6g fibre

serving suggestion Salad leaves or steamed green beans.

thai green prawn curry

Cook 2 tablespoons green curry paste in heated large deep frying pan, stirring, until fragrant. Add 500g (1 pound) shelled uncooked medium king prawns (shrimp), 150g (5 ounces) halved trimmed snow peas, 500g (1 pound) gai lan, cut into 5cm (2 inch) lengths, 2 teaspoons fish sauce, ½ cup water and 1⅔ cups coconut milk; bring to the boil, stirring. Reduce heat; simmer, uncovered, about 5 minutes or until prawns change colour and sauce thickens. Sprinkle with thai basil leaves to serve.

prep + cook time 10 minutes **serves** 4
nutritional count per serving 25.4g total fat (18.6g saturated fat); 1639kJ (392 cal); 7.8g carbohydrate; 30.9g protein; 5.4g fibre

serving suggestion Steamed jasmine rice.

harissa chicken burger

Combine 12 chicken tenderloins (900g) and 2 teaspoons harissa paste in medium bowl. Cook chicken in heated oiled large frying pan; season to taste. Meanwhile, split 4 hamburger buns in half; toast cut sides. Sandwich 60g (2 ounces) baby spinach leaves, 1 lebanese cucumber (130g), cut into ribbons, harissa chicken and ½ cup beetroot dip between buns.

prep + cook time 10 minutes **serves** 4
nutritional count per serving 7.7g total fat (1.9g saturated fat); 1802kJ (431 cal); 30.6g carbohydrate; 57g protein; 3.7g fibre

glazed fig bruschetta

Cut 6 medium figs in half; drizzle cut-sides with 2 tablespoons honey. Place figs, cut-side down, in heated large frying pan; cook until figs are warmed through. Add 1 tablespoon cold water to pan; remove from heat. Meanwhile, beat ⅔ cup thickened (heavy) cream and 1 tablespoon icing (confectioners') sugar in small bowl with electric mixer until soft peaks form. Beat in ⅓ cup mascarpone cheese. Toast four thick slices of brioche. Spread one side of each brioche with mascarpone mixture, top with fig halves.

prep + cook time 10 minutes **serves** 4
nutritional count per serving 30.8g total fat (18g saturated fat); 2370kJ (567 cal); 60.5g carbohydrate; 10.2g protein; 3.7g fibre

To make a strong espresso coffee, combine 2 tablespoons instant espresso coffee and 1 cup boiling water.

freeform tiramisu

½ cup (125ml) strong espresso coffee, cooled
½ cup (125ml) coffee-flavoured liqueur
10 sponge finger biscuits, halved crossways
⅔ cup (160ml) thickened (heavy) cream
¼ cup (40g) icing (confectioners') sugar
250g (8 ounces) mascarpone cheese

1 Combine coffee and ⅓ cup of the liqueur in small bowl. Dip biscuits, one at a time, into coffee mixture. Line four 1 cup (250ml) serving glasses with biscuits; drizzle with any remaining coffee mixture.
2 Beat cream and sifted icing sugar in small bowl with electric mixer until soft peaks form; beat in mascarpone and remaining liqueur. Divide mixture between glasses; dust with sifted cocoa, if you like.

prep time 10 minutes serves 4
nutritional count per serving 37g total fat (23.5g saturated fat); 2550kJ (610 cal); 47.4g carbohydrate; 8.6g protein; 0.4g fibre

You need about four passionfruit to get the amount of passionfruit pulp required for this recipe.

caramelised pineapple with coconut ice-cream

½ medium pineapple (1.25kg), cut into 12 slices
¼ cup (60ml) coconut-flavoured liqueur
2 cups (500g) vanilla ice-cream, softened slightly
½ cup (40g) desiccated coconut, toasted
⅓ cup (80ml) passionfruit pulp

1 Brush pineapple with 1 tablespoon of the liqueur. Pan-fry pineapple, in batches, in heated oiled large frying pan until caramelised and heated through.
2 Meanwhile, combine ice-cream, coconut and remaining liqueur in medium bowl.
3 Serve pineapple drizzled with passionfruit and topped with scoops of coconut ice-cream.

prep + cook time 10 minutes **serves** 4
nutritional count per serving 20g total fat
(14.4g saturated fat); 1873kJ (448 cal);
46.8g carbohydrate; 7.2g protein; 7.7g fibre

strawberry crush

500g (1 pound) strawberries, hulled, quartered
1 tablespoon orange-flavoured liqueur
2 tablespoons icing (confectioners') sugar
1¼ cups (310ml) thickened (heavy) cream,
  whipped (see note)
¾ cup (200g) yogurt
5 pavlova nests (50g), crumbled coarsely

1 Combine strawberries, liqueur and sifted icing sugar in medium bowl. Stand 5 minutes.
2 Meanwhile, combine cream, yogurt and pavlova nests in medium bowl.
3 Place half the cream mixture in four 1-cup (250ml) serving glasses. Top with half the strawberry mixture, then remaining cream mixture and strawberry mixture. Serve immediately.

prep time 10 minutes **serves** 4
nutritional count per serving 29.9g total fat (19.5g saturated fat); 1747kJ (418 cal); 27.2g carbohydrate; 6.4g protein; 2.8g fibre

note It is fine to use just 1 x 300ml carton of cream for this recipe.

This English dessert is often called Eton Mess, taking its name from Eton College, one of Britain's most famous public schools, where it was traditionally served. The 'mess' part is because it was all mixed together in one big bowl.

on the table in
15 minutes

ruby grapefruit, pomegranate and endive salad

3 ruby red grapefruit (1kg)
¼ cup (60ml) olive oil
2 tablespoons coarsely chopped fresh chervil
100g curly endive leaves
½ cup pomegranate pulp
½ cup (55g) coarsely chopped roasted walnuts

1 Juice half of one grapefruit; reserve juice. Peel remaining grapefruit; slice thickly.
2 To make dressing, combine reserved juice, oil and chervil in screw-top jar; shake well.
3 Toss endive and dressing in large bowl. Layer endive, grapefruit and pomegranate on serving plate; serve sprinkled with nuts.

prep time 15 minutes **serves** 4
nutritional count per serving 23.7g total fat (2.5g saturated fat); 1208kJ (289 cal); 12.8g carbohydrate; 4.5g protein; 4.6g fibre

note You need 1 medium pomegranate for this recipe. Pomegranate pulp consists of the seeds and the edible pulp surrounding them; it has a tangy sweet-sour flavour. To remove the seeds, cut the fruit in half crossways and hold each half cut-side down over a bowl. Hit the outside skin of the fruit sharply with a wooden spoon – as hard as you can – the seeds should fall out – if they don't, dig them out with a teaspoon.

pistachio and chilli crumbed chicken strips

1½ cups (105g) stale breadcrumbs
½ cup (70g) pistachios, roasted, chopped finely
1 fresh long red chilli, chopped finely
625g (1¼ pounds) chicken tenderloins
1 egg, beaten lightly
vegetable oil, for deep-frying

1 Combine breadcrumbs, nuts and chilli in medium shallow bowl. Dip chicken in egg, then in breadcrumb mixture to coat.
2 Meanwhile, heat oil in large deep saucepan. Deep-fry chicken, in batches, until cooked. Drain on absorbent paper; season to taste. Accompany with sweet chilli sauce, if you like.

prep + cook time 15 minutes serves 4
nutritional count per serving 26.5g total fat (4g saturated fat); 2098kJ (502 cal); 20.6g carbohydrate; 44.1g protein; 2.7g fibre

prawn and miso soup

200g (6½ ounces) soba noodles
6 x 18g (¾ ounce) sachets instant miso soup
400g (13 ounces) shelled uncooked medium
  prawns (shrimp)
90g (3 ounces) baby spinach leaves
3 green onions (scallions), sliced thinly
1 fresh long red chilli, sliced thinly

1 Cook noodles in large saucepan of boiling water
until tender; drain.
2 Meanwhile, combine soup sachets and 1.5 litres
(6 cups) water in large saucepan; bring to the boil.
Add prawns; cook until prawns change colour.
3 Stir in spinach, onion, chilli and noodles; serve
soup immediately.

prep + cook time 15 minutes **serves** 4
nutritional count per serving 3.2g total fat
(0.6g saturated fat); 1363kJ (326 cal);
41.2g carbohydrate; 30.3g protein; 4g fibre

note Miso is a thick bean paste made from
fermented soya beans and grains. It varies in
colour, texture and saltiness and is used for
flavouring soups, salad dressings and pickles.
Instant miso soup sachets are available from
Asian food stores and many larger supermarkets.

spiced chickpea and yogurt dip

800g (26 ounces) canned chickpeas (garbanzo),
  rinsed, drained
3 cloves garlic, crushed
¼ cup (60ml) lemon juice
⅔ cup (190g) yogurt
2 tablespoons tahini
½ teaspoon sumac

1 Cook chickpeas in medium saucepan of boiling water 2 minutes or until heated through. Drain, reserving ¼ cup of the cooking liquid.
2 Blend or process two thirds of the chickpeas with reserved cooking liquid, garlic, half the juice and 2 tablespoons of the yogurt until almost smooth. Season to taste.
3 Combine tahini, remaining juice and yogurt, and 2 tablespoons warm water in small bowl.
4 Spoon pureed chickpea mixture into serving bowl; sprinkle with whole chickpeas, then drizzle with yogurt mixture and sprinkle with sumac.

prep + cook time 15 minutes **serves** 4
nutritional count per serving 10.6g total fat (2.2g saturated fat); 1045kJ (250 cal); 21.6g carbohydrate; 13.1g protein; 8.1g fibre

serving suggestion Serve warm or cold with toasted pitta bread.

veal cutlets with pear and pistachio salsa

4 veal cutlets (500g)
1 small orange (180g)
2 medium pears (460g), unpeeled, chopped finely
¼ cup (35g) pistachios, roasted, chopped finely
⅓ cup finely chopped fresh flat-leaf parsley
1 tablespoon olive oil

1 Cook cutlets on heated oiled grill plate (or grill or barbecue).
2 Meanwhile, finely grate 1 teaspoon rind from orange. Squeeze juice from orange (you need ¼ cup juice).
3 To make salsa, combine rind and juice in medium bowl with remaining ingredients; season to taste. Serve cutlets topped with salsa.

prep + cook time 15 minutes **serves** 4
nutritional count per serving 11.4g total fat
(1.8g saturated fat); 1078kJ (258 cal);
12.3g carbohydrate; 24.7g protein; 3.5g fibre

zucchini and ricotta farfalle

375g (12 ounces) farfalle pasta
20 zucchini flowers with stem attached (400g)
1 medium lemon
30g (1 ounce) butter
200g (6½ ounces) ricotta cheese, crumbled
¼ cup coarsely chopped fresh chives

1   Cook pasta in large saucepan of boiling water
until tender; drain. Return pasta to pan.
2   Meanwhile, cut stems from zucchini flowers; chop
coarsely. Remove and discard stamens from flowers.
3   Finely grate 1 teaspoon rind from lemon. Squeeze
juice from lemon (you need ⅓ cup juice).
4   Melt butter in small frying pan; cook chopped
zucchini stems, stirring, until tender. Add zucchini
flowers, rind and juice; cook until wilted.
5   Gently stir zucchini mixture, cheese and chives
into pasta. Season to taste.

prep + cook time 15 minutes serves 4
nutritional count per serving 13.2g total fat
(7.8g saturated fat); 1952kJ (467 cal);
66.8g carbohydrate; 17.2g protein; 4.8g fibre

The stem of the zucchini is the baby zucchini attached to the flower.

mexican chicken wraps

16 chicken tenderloins (1.2kg)
35g (1 ounce) packet taco seasoning mix
8 large (26cm/10 inch) flour tortillas
1 large avocado (320g), mashed
2 cups shredded cos (romaine) lettuce leaves
2 large tomatoes (440g), chopped coarsely

1 Toss chicken in seasoning mix. Cook chicken on heated oiled grill plate (or grill or barbecue).
2 Meanwhile, warm tortillas according to packet directions.
3 Spread tortillas with avocado; top with lettuce, tomato and chicken. Roll wraps to enclose filling.

prep + cook time 15 minutes **serves** 4
nutritional count per serving 24.5g total fat
(5.3g saturated fat); 2884kJ (690 cal);
38g carbohydrate; 76.2g protein; 4.8g fibre

serving suggestion Sour cream and lime wedges.

40

mexican beef salad

35g (1 ounce) packet taco seasoning mix
600g (1¼ pound) piece beef rump steak
420g (13 ounces) canned four-bean mix,
  rinsed, drained
125g (4 ounces) canned corn kernels,
  rinsed, drained
2 large tomatoes (440g), chopped finely
½ cup coarsely chopped fresh coriander (cilantro)

1 Rub seasoning mix over both sides of steak. Cook steak in heated oiled large frying pan. Remove from pan; cover, stand 5 minutes then slice thickly.
2 Meanwhile, combine beans, corn, tomato and coriander in medium bowl; season to taste. Divide salad between serving plates; top with steak. Serve with lime wedges.

prep + cook time 15 minutes **serves** 4
nutritional count per serving 10.7g total fat
(4.6g saturated fat); 1392kJ (333 cal);
15.9g carbohydrate; 39.8g protein; 6.6g fibre

belgian mussels

3 medium tomatoes (450g), chopped coarsely
1½ cups (375ml) beer
¼ cup (60ml) sweet chilli sauce
2 cloves garlic, sliced thinly
1kg (2 pounds) cleaned black mussels
¼ cup coarsely chopped fresh flat-leaf parsley

1 Combine tomato, beer, sauce and garlic in large saucepan; bring to the boil, then simmer, uncovered, about 5 minutes or until tomato is soft.
2 Add mussels to pan; cook, covered, about 5 minutes or until mussels open (discard any that do not). Serve mussels with sauce.

prep + cook time 15 minutes **serves** 4
nutritional count per serving 1.5g total fat (0.4g saturated fat); 481kJ (115 cal); 9.4g carbohydrate; 7.8g protein; 2.5g fibre

serving suggestion Crusty bread.

warm salad of smoked salmon, spinach and potato

400g (13 ounces) baby new potatoes, quartered
2 tablespoons pouring cream
¼ cup (75g) mayonnaise
2 tablespoons finely chopped fresh dill
100g baby spinach leaves
200g sliced smoked salmon, chopped coarsely

1 Boil, steam or microwave potato until tender; drain. Cover to keep warm.
2 Meanwhile, make dressing by combining cream, mayonnaise and dill in small bowl.
3 Place warm potatoes in large bowl; season. Add spinach and salmon; stir gently.
4 Divide salad between serving plates; drizzle with dressing.

prep + cook time 15 minutes **serves** 4
nutritional count per serving 12.8g total fat (4g saturated fat); 1037kJ (248 cal); 17.1g carbohydrate; 14.8g protein; 2.8g fibre

Cover the ends of the bamboo skewers in foil to prevent them from scorching during cooking. Or, if you have time, soak them in cold water for 30 minutes before using.

mini lamb skewers with preserved lemon yogurt

500g (1 pound) diced lamb
2 tablespoons olive oil
2 teaspoons sumac
¾ cup (210g) greek-style yogurt
2 tablespoons finely chopped preserved lemon rind
2 tablespoons finely chopped fresh coriander
(cilantro)

1 Combine lamb, oil and sumac in medium bowl.
2 Thread lamb onto 12 bamboo skewers. Season. Cook skewers on heated oiled grill plate (or grill or barbecue).
3 Meanwhile, combine yogurt, lemon and coriander in small bowl. Serve skewers with lemon yogurt.

prep + cook time 15 minutes makes 12

nutritional count per skewer 7.3g total fat (2.5g saturated fat); 447kJ (107 cal); 0.9g carbohydrate; 9.6g protein; 0.1g fibre

serving suggestion Greek salad.

nasi goreng with pork

500g (1 pound) pork strips
1 large red capsicum (bell pepper) (350g),
  chopped coarsely
4 green onions (scallions), cut into 3cm lengths
60g (2 ounce) packet nasi goreng seasoning
3 cups (450g) cooked jasmine rice (see notes)
½ cup loosely packed fresh coriander leaves
  (cilantro)

1 Stir-fry pork, in batches, in heated oiled wok.
Remove from wok.
2 Add capsicum and onion to wok; stir-fry until just
tender. Add seasoning mix; stir-fry 1 minute. Add
rice, pork and coriander; stir-fry until heated through.

prep + cook time 15 minutes **serves** 4
nutritional count per serving 10.5g total fat
(3.4g saturated fat); 1672kJ (400 cal);
43.3g carbohydrate; 31.3g protein; 2.6g fibre

notes You need to cook 1 cup (200g) rice for this
recipe. Or, use two 250g sachets of pre-cooked
jasmine rice.
Nasi goreng seasoning is a spice paste found in
sachets in the Asian food section of supermarkets.

potato, fennel and caper salad

1kg (2 pounds) desiree potatoes, unpeeled, chopped coarsely
1 large fennel bulb (550g)
¼ cup (60ml) olive oil
2 tablespoons rinsed, drained baby capers
2 tablespoons lemon juice
2 teaspoons wholegrain (seeded) mustard

1 Boil, steam or microwave potato until tender; drain. Cover to keep warm.
2 Meanwhile, remove fronds from fennel; chop fronds coarsely. Thinly slice fennel bulb.
3 Heat 1 tablespoon of the oil in large frying pan; cook fennel, stirring, until tender. Place fennel in large bowl with potato, fennel fronds and capers.
4 To make dressing, combine juice, mustard and remaining oil in screw-top jar; shake well. Season to taste. Add dressing to salad; mix gently. Serve salad warm.

prep + cook time 15 minutes **serves** 6
nutritional count per serving 9.3g total fat (1.3g saturated fat); 798kJ (191 cal); 20.9g carbohydrate; 4g protein; 3.8g fibre

dukkah prawn skewers

1.2kg (2½ pounds) large uncooked king prawns
  (shrimp)
¼ cup (35g) pistachio dukkah
2 tablespoons olive oil
2 cloves garlic, crushed
2 teaspoons finely grated lemon rind

1 Shell and devein prawns, leaving tails intact.
2 Combine dukkah, oil, garlic and rind in large bowl; add prawns, toss to coat in dukkah mixture.
3 Thread prawns onto 8 bamboo skewers. Cook skewers on heated oiled grill plate (or grill or barbecue) until prawns change colour.

prep + cook time 15 minutes **serves** 4
nutritional count per serving 14.5g total fat
(2g saturated fat); 1124kJ (269 cal);
1.5g carbohydrate; 32.6g protein; 1.1g fibre

notes To save time, buy prawns already shelled from the fishmonger.
Dukkah is found in the spice aisle of supermarkets.
Cover the ends of the bamboo skewers in foil to prevent scorching during cooking. Or, if you have time, soak skewers in cold water for 30 minutes.

serving suggestion Mixed salad leaves and lemon wedges.

lamb cutlets in barbecue sauce and rosemary

12 french-trimmed lamb cutlets (880g)
½ cup (125ml) barbecue sauce
2 tablespoons finely chopped fresh rosemary
2 cloves garlic, crushed
2 tablespoons olive oil
400g (13 ounces) green beans, trimmed

1 Place cutlets in shallow dish; pour over combined sauce, rosemary, garlic and oil; season.
2 Cook cutlets on heated oiled grill plate (or grill or barbecue).
3 Meanwhile, boil, steam or microwave beans until tender; drain.
4 Serve cutlets with beans; season to taste.

prep + cook time 15 minutes **serves** 4
nutritional count per serving 28.2g total fat (9.9g saturated fat); 1793kJ (429 cal); 18.2g carbohydrate; 24.7g protein; 3.3g fibre

satay pork medallions

4 pork loin steaks (600g)
¼ cup (70g) crunchy peanut butter
⅓ cup (80ml) coconut cream
2 tablespoons sweet chilli sauce
2 teaspoons fish sauce
1 tablespoon coarsely chopped fresh coriander
  (cilantro)

1 Cook steaks on heated oiled grill plate (or grill or barbecue).
2 Meanwhile, combine peanut butter, coconut cream, sauces and ¼ cup water in small saucepan; cook, stirring, over heat about 3 minutes or until thickened slightly.
3 Serve steaks drizzled with sauce; sprinkle with coriander.

prep + cook time 15 minutes **serves** 4
nutritional count per serving 23.9g total fat (8.7g saturated fat); 1655kJ (396 cal); 4.6g carbohydrate; 39.7g protein; 2.8g fibre

serving suggestion Jasmine rice and steamed asian greens.

fried cauliflower

2 eggs
½ cup (110g) self-raising flour
½ cup (125ml) water
⅓ cup finely chopped fresh coriander (cilantro)
vegetable oil, for deep-frying
1 small cauliflower (1kg), cut into small florets
1 cup (280g) greek-style yogurt

1 To make batter, whisk eggs, flour and the water in medium shallow bowl until smooth. Stir in half the coriander; season.
2 Heat oil in wok. Dip cauliflower in batter; drain off excess. Deep-fry cauliflower, in batches, until browned lightly and tender. Drain on absorbent paper.
3 Combine remaining coriander and yogurt in small bowl; season to taste. Serve cauliflower with coriander yogurt.

prep + cook time 15 minutes serves 4
nutritional count per serving 9g total fat
(2.8g saturated fat); 1083kJ (259 cal);
27.4g carbohydrate; 14.2g protein; 5.2g fibre

grilled chicken with thai pineapple salad

625g (1¼ pounds) chicken thigh fillets
½ small pineapple (450g), chopped coarsely
½ cup loosely packed fresh mint leaves, torn
1 fresh long red chilli, sliced thinly
2 tablespoons lime juice
2 tablespoons fish sauce

1 Cook chicken on heated oiled grill plate (or grill or barbecue).
2 Meanwhile, combine remaining ingredients in small bowl. Serve chicken with salad.

prep + cook time 15 minutes **serves** 4
nutritional count per serving 11.4g total fat
(3.5g saturated fat); 1053kJ (252 cal);
5.6g carbohydrate; 30.8g protein; 1.9g fibre

smoky barbecue steaks

¼ cup (60ml) barbecue sauce
2 tablespoons tomato sauce
1 teaspoon smoked paprika
2 teaspoons cider vinegar
1 clove garlic, crushed
4 beef sirloin steaks (880g)

1   Combine sauces, paprika, vinegar and garlic in large bowl with steaks.
2   Cook steaks on heated oiled grill plate (or grill or barbecue), brushing frequently with marinade.

prep + cook time 15 minutes **serves** 4
nutritional count per serving 13.3g total fat (5.5g saturated fat); 1459kJ (349 cal); 10.1g carbohydrate; 46.7g protein; 0.5g fibre

serving suggestion Leafy green salad.

fresh summer salad

1 cup (280g) yogurt
2 teaspoons ground cumin
2 telegraph (hothouse) cucumbers (800g), halved
lengthways, seeded, sliced thickly
450g (14 ounces) canned pineapple pieces, drained
1 cup loosely packed fresh mint leaves
1 cup loosely packed fresh coriander leaves

1 Combine yogurt and cumin in small bowl;
season to taste.
2 Combine cucumber, pineapple, mint and
coriander in large bowl; season to taste.
3 Serve salad with yogurt.

prep time 15 minutes **serves** 4
nutritional count per serving 2.7g total fat
(1.6g saturated fat); 493kJ (118 cal);
15.1g carbohydrate; 6.1g protein; 4.2g fibre

Use fresh pineapple, if preferred.

chickpea and lentil salad

¾ cup sun-dried tomatoes (105g), drained,
  chopped coarsely
¼ cup (60ml) olive oil
1 tablespoon lemon juice
415g (13 ounces) canned brown lentils,
  rinsed, drained
410g (13 ounces) canned chickpeas (garbanzo),
  rinsed, drained
250g (8 ounces) silver beet (swiss chard),
  trimmed, shredded finely

1 To make dressing, blend or process ¼ cup of the
tomatoes, oil and juice until finely chopped.
2 Combine lentils, chickpeas, silver beet, half the
sun-dried tomato dressing and remaining sun-dried
tomatoes in large bowl; season to taste.
3 Top with remaining dressing.

prep time 15 minutes **serves** 4
nutritional count per serving 16.7g total fat
(2.3g saturated fat); 1325kJ (317 cal);
24.8g carbohydrate; 11.8g protein; 10.7g fibre

Spinach can be used in place of silver beet.

pine nut and dried fig couscous

1 cup (250ml) chicken stock
1 cup (200g) couscous
⅔ cup (130g) coarsely chopped dried figs
½ cup (80g) roasted pine nuts
2 teaspoons finely grated lemon rind
¼ cup (60ml) lemon juice
¼ cup finely chopped fresh flat-leaf parsley

1 Bring stock to the boil in medium saucepan. Remove from heat, add couscous, cover; stand about 5 minutes or until liquid is absorbed, fluffing with fork occasionally.
2 Stir remaining ingredients into couscous; season to taste.

prep + cook time 15 minutes **serves** 4
nutritional count per serving 9.9g total fat (0.7g saturated fat); 1179kJ (282 cal); 38.5g carbohydrate; 7.4g protein; 4.2g fibre

note Add your favourite dried fruit or nuts to the couscous. Serve warm or cold.

red onion salad with witlof and fetta

2 medium red onions (340g), cut into wedges
2 witlof (belgian endive) (250g), trimmed
1 cup loosely packed fresh mint leaves
200g (6½ ounces) crumbled fetta cheese
VINAIGRETTE
¼ cup (60ml) olive oil
2 tablespoons red wine vinegar

1 To make vinaigrette, combine oil and vinegar in screw-top jar; shake well, season to taste.
2 Combine onion, witlof, half the mint, half the cheese and half the vinaigrette in large bowl; season to taste.
3 Place salad on serving platter; top with remaining mint, fetta and vinaigrette.

prep time 15 minutes serves 4
nutritional count per serving 25.6g total fat
(9.6g saturated fat); 1262kJ (302 cal);
5.5g carbohydrate; 11.4g protein; 3.4g fibre

note Use soft goat's cheese in place of the fetta.

pear with blue cheese and prosciutto

baby cos with curried egg and chives

Cut 2 medium unpeeled pears into 6 wedges each; remove and discard core from each wedge. Sprinkle wedges with 2 teaspoons lemon juice. Cut 6 slices prosciutto in half lengthways. Press 150g crumbled blue cheese over prosciutto slices. Wrap prosciutto firmly around each pear wedge.

prep time 15 minutes **serves** 4
nutritional count per serving 13.6g total fat
(8.3g saturated fat); 895kJ (214 cal);
9.9g carbohydrate; 12g protein; 2.4g fibre

note Blue cheeses are mould-treated cheeses mottled with blue veining. Varieties include firm and crumbly stilton types to mild, creamy brie-like cheeses.

Combine 4 coarsely chopped hard-boiled eggs, ¼ cup mayonnaise, 1 teaspoon curry powder and 1 tablespoon finely chopped fresh chives in medium bowl; mash with fork until combined. Season to taste. Separate and wash leaves from 2 baby cos (romaine) lettuce. Place lettuce leaves on serving platter. Spoon egg mixture onto leaves; sprinkle with 1 tablespoon finely chopped fresh chives.

prep + cook time 15 minutes **serves** 4
nutritional count per serving 10g total fat
(2.1g saturated fat); 598kJ (143 cal);
4.5g carbohydrate; 8.1g protein; 2g fibre

chocolate rocky road ice-cream

Place 1-litre (4-cups) chocolate ice-cream in a microwave-safe bowl. Microwave on MEDIUM (50%) for 30 seconds or until just softened. Stir in 100g (3 ounces) finely chopped rocky road. Freeze 10 minutes. Meanwhile, stir 100g (3 ounces) coarsely chopped dark chocolate and ½ cup thickened (heavy) cream in small saucepan over low heat until smooth. Serve scoops of rocky road ice-cream drizzled with warm chocolate sauce. Sprinkle with extra 50g (1½ ounces) finely chopped rocky road to serve.

prep + cook time 15 minutes **serves** 4
nutritional count per serving 44.6g total fat (28.9g saturated fat); 2926kJ (700 cal); 66.3g carbohydrate; 9.8g protein; 1g fibre
note If you can't find rocky road confectionery, use a tub of chocolate rocky road ice-cream instead.

choc-cherry and hazelnut biscotti trifle

Combine 300g (10 ounces) thawed frozen pitted black cherries and ⅓ cup marsala in small bowl. Cut 4 thick slices biscotti from 170g (5½ ounces) chocolate hazelnut biscotti, then chop remaining biscotti coarsely. Place 6 x 62g (2 ounce) tubs chocolate mousse in medium bowl; whisk until smooth. Spoon half the cherry mixture into four 2-cup serving glasses; top with half the chopped biscotti and half the mousse. Repeat layering. Serve trifles with reserved biscotti slices.

prep time 15 minutes **serves** 4
nutritional count per serving 18.8g total fat (10.4g saturated fat); 1935kJ (463 cal); 56.4g carbohydrate; 10.1g protein; 2.4g fibre

mascarpone berry matchsticks

300g (10 ounces) frozen mixed berries
2 tablespoons citrus-flavoured liqueur
⅓ cup (55g) icing (confectioners') sugar
1 sheet butter puff pastry, thawed
200g (6½ ounces) mascarpone cheese
½ cup (125ml) thickened (heavy) cream

1 Place berries in medium bowl; sprinkle with liqueur and 1 tablespoon of the icing sugar.
2 Preheat oven to 220°C/425°F. Line oven tray with baking paper (parchment).
3 Cut pastry sheet into 8 rectangles. Place on oven tray. Dust pastry with 2 teaspoons of the sifted icing sugar. Bake about 10 minutes. Cool.
4 Beat mascarpone, cream and 2 tablespoons of the remaining sifted icing sugar in small bowl with electric mixer until soft peaks form.
5 Sandwich mascarpone mixture, berries and any berry juices between pastry slices. Dust matchsticks with remaining sifted icing sugar.

prep + cook time 15 minutes **serves** 4
nutritional count per serving 37.8g total fat
(23.3g saturated fat); 2391kJ (572 cal);
42.8g carbohydrate; 8g protein; 3.5g fibre

caramel banana split

½ cup (120g) caramel top 'n' fill
¾ cup (180ml) thickened (heavy) cream
4 small bananas (520g)
2 cups (500ml) vanilla ice-cream
2 tablespoons crushed peanuts
8 slices almond bread (30g)

1 Whisk caramel and ¼ cup of the cream in small saucepan over low heat until smooth.
2 Beat remaining cream in small bowl with electric mixer until soft peaks form.
3 Peel then cut bananas lengthways; place in serving dishes. Top bananas with ice-cream and whipped cream; drizzle with sauce and sprinkle with nuts. Serve banana split with almond bread.

prep + cook time 15 minutes **serves** 4
nutritional count per serving 32.4g total fat (19.5g saturated fat); 2383kJ (570 cal); 60g carbohydrate; 10.1g protein; 2.5g fibre

Caramel top 'n' fill is a delicious caramel made from milk and cane sugar. Use it straight from the can for slices, tarts and cheesecakes.

on the table in 25 minutes

warm tuna and green tea noodle salad

2 x 10cm (4 inch) sticks fresh lemon grass (40g),
  chopped finely
1 tablespoon light soy sauce
2 teaspoons grated palm sugar
2 tablespoons lime juice
3 x 155g (5 ounces) tuna steaks
200g (6½ ounces) dried green tea soba noodles
2 teaspoons sesame oil
1 cup firmly packed fresh coriander leaves
  (cilantro)

1 Blend or process lemon grass, sauce, sugar and
1 tablespoon of the juice until smooth.
2 Combine tuna and half the lemon grass mixture
in large bowl. Cook tuna on heated oiled grill plate
(or grill or barbecue). Cover tuna; stand 5 minutes
then slice thinly.
3 Meanwhile, cook noodles in large saucepan
of boiling water until tender; drain.
4 Whisk remaining lemon grass mixture, oil and
remaining juice in large bowl. Add tuna, noodles
and coriander; mix gently. Season to taste.

prep + cook time 25 minutes **serves** 4
nutritional count per serving 9.5g total fat
(3.1g saturated fat); 1584kJ (379 cal);
36g carbohydrate; 35.4g protein; 2.4g fibre

note You can use brown sugar instead of the
palm sugar.

Green tea soba noodles are flavoured with
powdered green tea and are available from
Asian food stores and the Asian food section
of most large supermarkets. Use plain dried
soba noodles if you prefer.

White balsamic vinegar is available from most major supermarkets. Use white wine vinegar if you prefer.

prawn and mango salad

1kg (2 pounds) cooked medium king prawns (shrimp)
1 medium mango (430g), sliced thinly
2 baby cos (romaine) lettuce, leaves separated
¼ cup coarsely chopped fresh chives
2 tablespoons olive oil
1 tablespoon white balsamic vinegar

1 Shell and devein prawns, leaving tails intact.
2 Combine prawns and remaining ingredients in large bowl; season to taste.

prep time 25 minutes serves 4
nutritional count per serving 10.3g total fat (1.4g saturated fat); 1066kJ (255 cal); 11.3g carbohydrate; 27.7g protein; 3.1g fibre

note To save time, buy shelled prawns from the fishmonger.

sticky turkey sang choy bow

375g (12 ounces) minced (ground) turkey
1 tablespoon kecap manis
1 tablespoon light brown sugar
1 tablespoon light soy sauce
4 small iceberg lettuce leaves
1 fresh long red chilli, sliced thinly

1   Stir-fry mince in heated oiled wok until mince changes colour. Add kecap manis, sugar and sauce; stir-fry until mixture is sticky and slightly dry. Season to taste.
2   Divide mince mixture between lettuce leaves; sprinkle with chilli.

prep + cook time 25 minutes **serves** 4
nutritional count per serving 4g total fat
(1g saturated fat); 539kJ (129 cal);
3.5g carbohydrate; 19.5g protein; 0.1g fibre

Commercial laksa pastes vary dramatically in their heat intensity so, while we call for ⅓ cup here, you might try using less of the laksa paste you've purchased until you can determine how hot it makes the final dish.

chicken laksa

400g (13 ounces) chicken thigh fillets, sliced thinly
⅓ cup (100g) laksa paste
1½ cups (375ml) chicken stock
½ cup (125ml) water
1 cup (250ml) coconut milk
200g (6½ ounces) bean thread noodles
½ cup loosely packed fresh coriander
  (cilantro) leaves

1 Cook chicken in heated oiled large saucepan, in batches, until browned lightly. Remove from pan.
2 Cook paste in same pan, stirring, about 3 minutes or until fragrant. Return chicken to pan with stock, the water and coconut milk; bring to the boil. Reduce heat; simmer, uncovered, about 10 minutes or until chicken is cooked. Season to taste.
3 Meanwhile, place noodles in medium heatproof bowl, cover with boiling water; stand until noodles are tender, then drain.
4 Divide noodles between serving bowls; ladle over hot laksa. Serve sprinkled with coriander.

prep + cook time 25 minutes serves 4
nutritional count per serving 29.6g total fat
(15.4g saturated fat); 1789kJ (428 cal);
15.8g carbohydrate; 23.4g protein; 4.3g fibre

note It's fine to use a whole 270ml can of coconut milk.

peking duck salad

2 x 155g (5 ounces) duck breast fillets, skin on
2 tablespoons hoisin sauce
1 lebanese cucumber (130g)
2 tablespoons lime juice
90g (3 ounces) baby asian greens
4 green onions (scallions), finely sliced

1 Brush duck all over with half the sauce. Cook duck in heated oiled medium frying pan, skin-side down, about 5 minutes or until skin is crisp. Turn duck; cook a further 5 minutes or until cooked as desired. Cover duck; stand 5 minutes then slice thinly.
2 Meanwhile, using vegetable peeler, slice cucumber lengthways into thin ribbons.
3 Whisk juice and the remaining sauce in large bowl. Add duck, cucumber, asian greens and onions; mix gently. Season to taste.

prep + cook time 25 minutes **serves** 4
nutritional count per serving 29.4g total fat (8.7g saturated fat); 1392kJ (333 cal); 5.8g carbohydrate; 11.3g protein; 2.1g fibre

garlic prawn and noodle salad

750g (1½ pounds) uncooked medium king prawns
  (shrimp)
2 cloves garlic, crushed
125g (4 ounces) rice vermicelli
1 medium lemon (140g)
155g (5 ounces) snow peas, trimmed,
  sliced thinly lengthways
⅓ cup finely chopped fresh mint

1   Shell and devein prawns, leaving tails intact.
Combine prawns and garlic in medium bowl.
Cook prawns on heated oiled grill plate (or grill
or barbecue) until changed in colour.
2   Meanwhile, place vermicelli in medium heatproof
bowl, cover with boiling water; stand until vermicelli
is tender, then drain.
3   Finely grate 2 teaspoons rind from lemon. Squeeze
juice from lemon (you need 2 tablespoons juice).
4   Combine prawns, noodles, rind, juice, peas and
mint in large bowl; season to taste.

prep + cook time 25 minutes **serves** 4
nutritional count per serving 0.9g total fat
(0.1g saturated fat); 564kJ (135 cal);
9.2g carbohydrate; 21.3g protein; 1.7g fibre

smoked salmon spaghetti with pea pesto

375g (12 ounces) spaghettini pasta
2 cups (240g) frozen peas
¾ cup firmly packed fresh mint leaves
2 tablespoons roasted pine nuts
2 tablespoons lemon juice
200g (6½ ounces) smoked salmon, sliced thinly

1 Cook pasta in large saucepan of boiling water until tender; drain.
2 Meanwhile, boil, steam or microwave peas until tender; drain, reserving ½ cup cooking liquid.
3 To make pea pesto, blend or process peas, reserved cooking liquid, mint, nuts and juice until mixture is smooth.
4 Combine hot pasta, pea pesto and salmon in large bowl; season to taste. Sprinkle with fresh mint leaves.

prep + cook time 25 minutes **serves** 4
nutritional count per serving 8.8g total fat (1g saturated fat); 2002kJ (479 cal); 68.4g carbohydrate; 26.8g protein; 7.6g fibre

chilli jam beef noodles

250g (8 ounces) dried rice stick noodles
625g (1¼ pounds) beef eye fillet, sliced thinly
2 tablespoons thai chilli jam
1 medium red capsicum (bell pepper) (200g),
  sliced thinly
155g (5 ounces) sugar snap peas, trimmed
½ cup loosely packed thai basil leaves

1 Place noodles in large heatproof bowl, cover
with boiling water; stand until tender, drain.
2 Meanwhile, combine beef and half the chilli jam
in medium bowl.
3 Stir-fry beef, in batches, in heated oiled wok
until browned; remove from wok.
4 Add capsicum to wok; stir-fry until tender. Return
beef to wok with noodles, peas, ¼ cup water and
remaining chilli jam; stir-fry until hot. Season to
taste; serve sprinkled with basil.

prep + cook time 25 minutes serves 4
nutritional count per serving 9.9g total fat
(4g saturated fat); 1195kJ (286 cal);
12.2g carbohydrate; 35.6g protein; 2.1g fibre

notes Thai basil, also known as horapa, has a slight
licorice or aniseed taste. Use sweet basil if thai basil
is unavailable.
Thai chilli jam is a combination of garlic, shallots, chilli,
tomato paste, fish sauce, galangal, spices and shrimp
paste, it is sold under various names, and can be
found in the Asian food section of the supermarket.

roasted beetroot and orange salad

1kg (2 pounds) baby beetroots (beets), trimmed
2 medium oranges (480g)
75g (2½ ounces) baby spinach leaves
½ cup (55g) coarsely chopped roasted walnuts
1 tablespoon white wine vinegar
2 teaspoons caraway seeds

1 Preheat oven to 240°C/475°F.
2 Wrap beetroot individually in foil; place in small shallow baking dish. Roast about 20 minutes or until tender. When cool enough to handle, peel and halve beetroot.
3 Meanwhile, segment oranges over small bowl; reserve ¼ cup juice.
4 Combine beetroot, orange segments, reserved juice and remaining ingredients in large bowl; season to taste.

prep + cook time 25 minutes **serves** 4
nutritional count per serving 9.9g total fat
(0.6g saturated fat); 1032kJ (247 cal);
27.1g carbohydrate; 7.6g protein; 9.9g fibre

Use gloves when peeling beetroot to stop the juice from staining your hands.

lemon pepper pork with broad bean salad

4 pork cutlets (940g)
2 tablespoons lemon pepper seasoning
2 cups (360g) frozen broad (fava) beans
1 medium lemon
100g (3½ ounces) fetta cheese, crumbled
¾ cup fresh mint leaves, torn

1 Sprinkle cutlets both sides with seasoning; cook on heated oiled grill plate (or grill or barbecue).
2 Meanwhile, boil, steam or microwave beans until just tender; drain. When cool enough to handle, peel beans.
3 Finely grate 2 teaspoons rind from lemon. Squeeze juice from lemon (you need 2 tablespoons juice).
4 Combine beans, rind, juice, cheese and mint in large bowl. Season to taste. Serve cutlets with salad.

prep + cook time 25 minutes **serves** 4
nutritional count per serving 24.1g total fat (10g saturated fat); 1685kJ (403 cal); 2.6g carbohydrate; 41.2g protein; 6.3g fibre

barbecued honey mustard pork cutlets

880g (1¾ pounds) french-trimmed pork cutlets
2 tablespoons peanut oil
2 tablespoons honey
2 tablespoons dijonnaise
60g (2 ounces) mixed salad leaves
1 large pear (330g), unpeeled, cut into long
  thin strips

1 Combine cutlets, oil, honey and dijonnaise in
large bowl; season.
2 Cook cutlets on heated oiled grill plate (or grill
or barbecue).
3 Combine salad leaves and pear in medium bowl.
Serve salad with cutlets.

prep + cook time 25 minutes **serves** 4
nutritional count per serving 26.2g total fat
(7.1g saturated fat); 1777kJ (425 cal);
19.9g carbohydrate; 26.8g protein; 2.2g fibre

notes We used red sensation pears to add colour
to the dish. They have a distinctive red and gold
tone and a sweet, buttery flesh.
Pork loin chops are also suitable for this recipe.

The cutlets can be marinated, covered, in the
refrigerator, for 2 hours or overnight.

chicken and pea pilaf

625g (1¼ pounds) chicken thigh fillets,
  chopped coarsely
1½ cups (300g) white long-grain rice
1½ cups (375ml) chicken stock
¾ cup (180ml) water
1 cup (120g) frozen peas
½ cup coarsely chopped fresh flat-leaf parsley
¼ cup (35g) roasted slivered almonds

1 Cook chicken in heated oiled large saucepan, in batches, until browned.

2 Return chicken to pan with rice, stock and the water; bring to the boil. Reduce heat; simmer, covered tightly, 5 minutes. Sprinkle peas over rice; simmer, covered tightly, about 10 minutes or until rice is tender and liquid is absorbed.

3 Remove from heat; stand, covered, 5 minutes. Stir in parsley; season to taste. Serve pilaf sprinkled with nuts.

prep + cook time 25 minutes **serves** 4
nutritional count per serving 17g total fat
(4g saturated fat); 2362kJ (565 cal);
62.1g carbohydrate; 38.7g protein; 3.5g fibre

caprese tarts

2 sheets puff pastry
3 medium tomatoes (450g), sliced thinly
6 bocconcini cheese (360g), sliced thinly
1 tablespoon balsamic glaze
⅓ cup coarsely chopped fresh basil
⅓ cup (25g) shaved parmesan cheese

1 Preheat oven to 220°C/425°F. Oil oven trays.
2 Cut pastry sheets in half; place pastry on trays.
Fold edges of pastry over to make 1cm (½ inch)
borders; press down firmly, prick bases with fork.
Bake about 15 minutes or until browned lightly.
Press centres with the back of a spatula to flatten.
3 Top pastry with tomato and bocconcini; bake
about 3 minutes or until cheese melts. Season.
4 Serve tarts drizzled with balsamic glaze; sprinkle
with basil and parmesan.

prep + cook time 25 minutes **serves** 4
nutritional count per serving 34.8g total fat
(11.6g saturated fat); 2261kJ (541 cal);
32.2g carbohydrate; 23.8g protein; 2.7g fibre

soy and citrus fish parcels

1 fresh small red thai (serrano) chilli, chopped finely
4 x 155g (5 ounces) firm white fish fillets
1 medium lemon (140g), sliced thinly
2 tablespoons light soy sauce
1 teaspoon sesame oil
2 green onions (scallions), sliced thinly

1 Preheat oven to 200°C/400°F.
2 Sprinkle chilli all over fish. Place each fish on a 30cm (12 inch) square of baking paper (parchment); top with lemon, drizzle with combined sauce and oil. Gather corners of paper together; fold to enclose. Place parcels on oven tray; bake about 15 minutes.
3 Serve fish parcels sprinkled with onion.

prep + cook time 25 minutes **serves** 4
nutritional count per serving 4.6g total fat (1.2g saturated fat); 727kJ (174 cal); 0.5g carbohydrate; 32.3g protein; 0.1g fibre

serving suggestion Steamed baby pak choy and jasmine rice.

note We used snapper fillets for this recipe.

cranberry-glazed turkey with kumara mash

1kg (2 pounds) kumara (orange sweet potato),
  chopped coarsely
2 tablespoons pine nuts, roasted
¼ cup (80g) cranberry sauce
4 x 125g (4 ounces) turkey breast steaks
¼ cup (35g) dried cranberries
½ cup (125ml) water
⅓ cup coarsely chopped fresh coriander (cilantro)

1   Boil, steam or microwave kumara until tender;
drain. Mash kumara until smooth; season to taste,
cover to keep warm.
2   Brush most of the sauce all over turkey; cook
turkey in heated oiled large frying pan. Remove
from pan; cover to keep warm.
3   Add remaining sauce, cranberries and the water
to same pan; bring to the boil. Boil until liquid is
thickened slightly. Remove from heat; stir in nuts
and coriander, season to taste.
4   Serve turkey with kumara mash and sauce.

prep + cook time 25 minutes **serves** 4
nutritional count per serving 9.5g total fat
(1.3g saturated fat); 1693kJ (405 cal);
44.5g carbohydrate; 32.3g protein; 4.9g fibre

serving suggestion Steamed green beans or
a green salad.

You need to buy a whole barbecue chicken weighing about 800g for this recipe.

chicken, pumpkin and sage lasagne stacks

3 fresh lasagne sheets (145g)
125g (4 ounces) butter, chopped coarsely
375g (12 ounces) pumpkin, chopped finely
185g (6 ounces) asparagus, trimmed,
  chopped coarsely
2 cups (320g) shredded barbecued chicken
12 fresh sage leaves

1 Cut each lasagne sheet into quarters. Cook pasta, in batches, in large saucepan of boiling water until tender; drain. Place pasta sheets, in single layer, on tray; cover to keep warm.
2 Meanwhile, heat one-quarter of the butter in large frying pan; cook pumpkin, stirring, about 5 minutes or until almost tender. Add asparagus; cook, stirring, about 5 minutes or until vegetables are tender. Add chicken; cook, stirring, until hot; season to taste. Remove chicken mixture from pan; cover to keep warm.
3 Heat remaining butter in same pan until browned lightly. Add sage; remove from heat.
4 Place one pasta sheet on each of four serving plates. Top with half the chicken mixture then another pasta sheet. Repeat with remaining chicken mixture and pasta. Drizzle with sage butter.

prep + cook time 25 minutes **serves** 4
nutritional count per serving 31.6g total fat (18.7g saturated fat); 1718kJ (411 cal); 8.4g carbohydrate; 23.1g protein; 1.8g fibre

barbecued salmon with minted peas and beans

2 limes
4 x 155g (5 ounces) salmon fillets
155g (5 ounces) green beans, trimmed,
  chopped coarsely
1 cup (120g) frozen peas
⅓ cup finely chopped fresh mint
½ cup (125ml) buttermilk

1 Finely grate 2 teaspoons rind from limes; squeeze
juice from limes (you need 1 tablespoon juice).
2 Rub salmon all over with rind; cook salmon on
heated oiled grill plate (or grill or barbecue).

3 Meanwhile, boil, steam or microwave beans
and peas, separately, until tender; drain. Combine
beans, peas and half the mint in medium bowl;
season to taste.
4 Combine buttermilk, juice and remaining mint
in small jug; season to taste.
5 Serve bean mixture with fish; drizzle with
buttermilk dressing.

prep + cook time 25 minutes **serves** 4
nutritional count per serving 11.9g total fat
(2.9g saturated fat); 1129kJ (270 cal);
4.7g carbohydrate; 34.4g protein; 3.1g fibre

cajun chicken with lime hollandaise

2 tablespoons cajun seasoning
4 x 155g (5 ounces) chicken breast fillets,
  halved lengthways
2 tablespoons lime juice
2 egg yolks
200g (6½ ounces) butter, melted
125g (4 ounces) rocket (arugula)

1 Rub seasoning all over chicken; cook chicken on heated oiled grill plate (or grill or barbecue), in batches, until cooked through.
2 Meanwhile, to make lime hollandaise, blend or process juice and egg yolks until combined. With motor operating, gradually add hot butter in a thin, steady stream; process until hollandaise is smooth and thick, season to taste.
3 Serve chicken with lime hollandaise and rocket.

prep + cook time 25 minutes **serves** 4
nutritional count per serving 47.6g total fat (28.8g saturated fat); 2424kJ (580 cal); 1.2g carbohydrate; 37.8g protein; 0.5g fibre

penne with vegetable bolognese and ricotta sauce

375g (12 ounces) penne pasta
1 small red onion (100g), chopped finely
1 small red capsicum (bell pepper) (150g),
  chopped finely
2 fresh small red thai (serrano) chillies, sliced thinly
2 tablespoons finely chopped fresh basil
400g (13 ounces) bottled ricotta pasta sauce

1 Cook pasta in large saucepan of boiling water until tender; drain. Return pasta to pan.
2 Meanwhile, heat oiled large frying pan; cook onion, capsicum, chilli and basil until vegetables are softened.
3 Add pasta sauce to vegetable mixture; bring to the boil. Combine sauce mixture with pasta; season to taste.
4 Serve pasta topped with fresh basil leaves and flaked parmesan, if you like.

prep + cook time 25 minutes **serves** 4
nutritional count per serving 6.8g total fat (3.2g saturated fat); 1881kJ (450 cal); 71.4g carbohydrate; 22.3g protein; 4.7g fibre

note Use your favourite bottled pasta cheese sauce in this recipe, if you prefer.

harissa lamb with orange couscous

410g (13 ounces) lamb backstraps
1 tablespoon harissa paste
1 teaspoon ground cumin
2 medium oranges (480g)
1½ cups (300g) couscous
1½ cups (375ml) boiling water
½ cup coarsely chopped fresh mint

1 Combine lamb, harissa and cumin in medium bowl; cook lamb on heated oiled grill plate (or grill or barbecue). Remove from pan, cover lamb; stand 5 minutes then slice thinly.
2 Meanwhile, finely grate 2 teaspoons rind from oranges; segment oranges over small bowl, reserving 2 tablespoons juice.
3 Combine couscous, rind and the water in large heatproof bowl, cover; stand about 5 minutes or until water is absorbed, fluffing with fork occasionally. Stir in orange segments, reserved juice and mint; season to taste.
4 Serve couscous with lamb.

prep + cook time 25 minutes **serves** 4
nutritional count per serving 9.8g total fat
(4.2g saturated fat); 2048kJ (490 cal);
65.8g carbohydrate; 32.2g protein; 3.1g fibre

asparagus and zucchini rice

¾ cup (180ml) chicken consommé
1 large zucchini (150g), chopped coarsely
185g (6 ounces) asparagus, trimmed,
  chopped coarsely
500g (1 pound) pre-cooked brown medium-grain rice
2 tablespoons finely chopped fresh flat-leaf parsley
1 cup (80g) finely grated parmesan cheese

1   Combine consommé, zucchini and asparagus in deep frying pan; bring to the boil, simmer, uncovered, until liquid is reduced by half.
2   Add rice and parsley; cook, stirring, until hot. Stir in cheese; season to taste. Serve topped with extra parmesan.

prep + cook time 25 minutes **serves** 4
nutritional count per serving 5.4g total fat (3g saturated fat); 840kJ (201 cal); 27.6g carbohydrate; 9.2g protein; 2.2g fibre

notes You can use vegetable stock instead of the chicken consommé.
Stir a little chopped preserved lemon and fresh tarragon into the rice, if you like.

spicy squid and tomato linguine

375g (12 ounces) linguine pasta
2 cloves garlic, crushed
1 teaspoon dried chilli flakes
800g (28 ounces) canned crushed tomatoes
500g (1 pound) cleaned squid hoods, sliced thinly
30g (1 ounce) baby rocket leaves (arugula)

1 Cook pasta in large saucepan of boiling water until tender; drain.
2 Meanwhile, cook garlic and chilli flakes in heated oiled large frying pan, stirring, until fragrant. Add undrained tomatoes; bring to the boil. Reduce heat; simmer, uncovered, about 10 minutes or until sauce thickens slightly.
3 Add squid to tomato sauce; cook, stirring occasionally, about 5 minutes or until squid is tender. Season to taste.
4 Combine hot pasta and sauce; serve with rocket.

prep + cook time 25 minutes **serves** 4
nutritional count per serving 3g total fat (0.7g saturated fat); 1919kJ (459 cal); 70.5g carbohydrate; 33.3g protein; 5.9g fibre

89

tandoori lamb racks

Preheat oven to 240°C/475°F. Brush ⅓ cup tandoori paste all over 4 x 3-cutlet (760g) french-trimmed lamb racks; place lamb on oiled wire rack over large baking dish. Roast about 20 minutes. Meanwhile, combine ¾ cup basmati rice, ½ cup chicken stock and ½ cup water in medium saucepan; bring to the boil. Reduce heat; simmer, tightly covered, about 10 minutes or until rice is tender and liquid absorbed. Remove from heat; stand, covered, 5 minutes. Stir in ⅓ cup finely chopped fresh coriander (cilantro); season to taste. Serve lamb with rice, ½ cup yogurt and some lime wedges.

prep + cook time 25 minutes **serves** 4
nutritional count per serving 21.5g total fat (7.5g saturated fat); 1735kJ (415 cal); 33.3g carbohydrate; 20.9g protein; 2.9g fibre

prawn lettuce cups

Shell and devein 500g (1 pound) cooked medium king prawns (shrimp); chop prawn meat coarsely. Combine prawns, 1 coarsely chopped medium avocado, ¼ cup coarsely chopped fresh coriander (cilantro), 1 tablespoon sweet chilli sauce and 1 tablespoon lime juice in medium bowl; season to taste. Divide prawn mixture between 12 small butter (boston) lettuce leaves. Serve with sweet chilli sauce, if you like.

prep time 25 minutes **makes** 12
nutritional count per cup 10.4g total fat (2.2g saturated fat); 656kJ (157 cal); 1.3g carbohydrate; 13.9g protein; 1.3g fibre

note To save time, buy shelled prawns from the fishmonger.

last-minute trifles

Divide a coarsely chopped 125g (4 ounce) sponge cake between six ¾-cup (180ml) serving glasses; drizzle ¼ cup sweet sherry over the sponge. Whip 1¼ cups (310ml) thickened (heavy) cream (see note) until soft peaks form. Thinly slice 125g (4 ounces) strawberries. Coarsely chop 3 x 155g (5 ounce) raspberry-flavoured jelly (jello) cups. Top sponge with ½ cup thick custard, jelly, the cream, then the strawberries.

prep time 25 minutes **serves** 6
nutritional count per serving 20.2g total fat
(13g saturated fat); 1413kJ (338 cal);
31.6g carbohydrate; 4.9g protein; 0.7g fibre

note It is fine to use just 1 x 300ml carton of cream for this recipe.

barbecued fruit salad

Slice cheeks from 2 medium mangoes; remove flesh in one piece from skin using a large spoon. Cut each cheek into three pieces. Quarter 2 medium bananas and 3 kiwifruit. Thickly slice half a peeled small pineapple. Cook fruit, in batches, on heated oiled grill plate (or grill or barbecue) until browned lightly and tender. Meanwhile, combine ½ cup passionfruit-flavoured yogurt and 1 tablespoon lime juice in small bowl. Serve fruit with lime and passionfruit yogurt.

prep + cook time 25 minutes **serves** 6
nutritional count per serving 1g total fat
(0.4g saturated fat); 669kJ (160 cal);
31.3g carbohydrate; 3.8g protein; 4.5g fibre

apple salad with lemon ice

4 large green apples (800g), unpeeled,
  sliced thinly
2 cups ice cubes
2 tablespoons icing (confectioners') sugar
¼ cup firmly packed fresh mint leaves
2 tablespoons lemon juice

1 Stack apple on serving plates.
2 Blend or process ice cubes, icing sugar, mint and juice until fine.
3 Sprinkle lemon ice over apples.

prep time 25 minutes **serves** 6
nutritional count per serving 0.1g total fat
(0g saturated fat); 293kJ (70 cal);
15.4g carbohydrate; 0.4g protein; 2.2g fibre

berry hazelnut cups

250g (8 ounces) raspberries
2 tablespoons icing (confectioners') sugar
1¼ cups (310ml) thickened (heavy) cream (see note)
2 tablespoons hazelnut-flavoured liqueur
90g packet brandy baskets
⅓ cup (45g) coarsely chopped roasted hazelnuts

1 Blend or process half the raspberries and half the icing sugar until smooth; strain through a fine sieve into small jug.
2 Beat cream, remaining icing sugar and liqueur in small bowl with electric mixer until soft peaks form.
3 Divide cream between brandy baskets; top with remaining raspberries and nuts. Drizzle with raspberry sauce.

prep time 25 minutes **serves** 6
nutritional count per serving 40.4g total fat (23.5g saturated fat); 2174kJ (520 cal); 26.9g carbohydrate; 4.7g protein; 5.4g fibre

note It is fine to use 1 x 300ml carton of cream for this recipe.

You need 6 brandy baskets for this recipe.

on the table in 35 minutes

garlic prawns with steamed rice

1 cup (200g) white long-grain rice
1kg (2 pounds) uncooked king prawns (shrimp)
4 cloves garlic, crushed
½ cup (125ml) dry white wine
1¼ cups (310ml) pouring cream (see notes)
¼ cup finely chopped fresh chives

1 Rinse rice in strainer under cold running water until water runs clear; drain. Place rice in medium saucepan with 1 cup water, cover; bring to the boil then simmer about 8 minutes or until rice is tender. Stand, covered, 3 minutes, then fluff rice with fork.
2 Meanwhile, shell and devein prawns, leaving tails intact.
3 Heat oiled large frying pan; cook prawns and garlic, stirring, until prawns change colour. Add wine, simmer, uncovered, until liquid is reduced by half.
4 Add cream to pan; simmer, uncovered, until mixture is thickened slightly. Season to taste.
5 Sprinkle prawn mixture with chives; serve with rice.

prep + cook time 35 minutes **serves** 4
nutritional count per serving 33.5g total fat
(21.6g saturated fat); 2567kJ (614 cal);
42.1g carbohydrate; 30.7g protein; 1g fibre

notes It is fine to use 1 x 300ml carton of cream for this recipe.
Prawns and garlic can be combined in a bowl and refrigerated, covered, for 2 hours for extra flavour.

sun-dried tomato and goat's cheese pizza

1 cup (150g) sun-dried tomatoes in oil, drained
2 large (30cm/12 inch) round thin pizza bases
½ cup (75g) seeded black olives, halved
2 chorizo sausages (345g), sliced thinly
½ cup fresh basil leaves, shredded finely
220g (7 ounces) goat's cheese, crumbled

1 Preheat oven to 220°C/425°F.
2 Blend or process tomatoes until almost smooth; spread over pizza bases leaving a 1cm (½ inch) border on each. Place bases on oven trays.
3 Top bases with olives, chorizo, half the basil and half the cheese. Bake about 15 minutes or until base is crisp; season.
4 Serve pizza sprinkled with remaining basil and cheese.

prep + cook time 35 minutes serves 4
nutritional count per serving 42.5g total fat (16.1g saturated fat); 4251kJ (1017 cal); 109g carbohydrate; 43.2g protein; 12.4g fibre

spaghetti with meatballs and cherry tomatoes

750g (1½ pounds) beef sausages
250g (8 ounces) cherry tomatoes, quartered
400g (13 ounces) bottled tomato pasta sauce
¼ cup coarsely chopped fresh basil
375g (12 ounces) spaghetti
½ cup (40g) finely grated parmesan cheese

1 Squeeze meat from sausages; roll meat into balls.
2 Cook meatballs in oiled large frying pan until browned all over. Add tomato, sauce and half the basil. Bring to the boil; simmer, uncovered, about 5 minutes or until meatballs are cooked through. Season to taste.

3 Meanwhile, cook spaghetti in large saucepan of boiling water until tender; drain.
4 Combine sauce mixture, spaghetti and half the cheese in large bowl. Serve sprinkled with remaining basil and cheese.

prep + cook time 35 minutes **serves** 4
nutritional count per serving 52.7g total fat (25.2g saturated fat); 4009kJ (959 cal); 78.7g carbohydrate; 37.8g protein; 10.8g fibre

notes Use flavoured sausages instead of plain. If you prefer, cook the sausages whole then slice and add to the tomato mixture.

char-grilled baby octopus and artichoke salad

1 cup loosely packed fresh dill
1kg (2 pounds) baby octopus, cleaned, halved
¼ cup (60ml) mustard seed oil
2 teaspoons finely grated lemon rind
¼ cup (60ml) lemon juice
500g (1 pound) marinated artichokes, drained

1   Coarsely chop half the dill; combine in large
bowl with octopus, oil, rind and juice; season.
2   Cook octopus on heated oiled grill plate (or grill
or barbecue) about 2 minutes or until tender.
3   Combine octopus with artichokes and remaining
dill in large bowl; season to taste.

prep + cook time 35 minutes **serves** 4
nutritional count per serving 18.6g total fat
(2.7g saturated fat); 1881kJ (450 cal);
4g carbohydrate; 65.3g protein; 2.5g fibre

prawn cocktail in fillo pastry

5 sheets fillo pastry (see notes)
50g (1½ ounces) butter, melted
1kg (2 pounds) cooked king prawns (shrimp)
1 cup (60g) firmly packed thinly shredded
  iceberg lettuce
1 small red onion (100g), sliced finely
½ cup (125ml) seafood cocktail sauce

1 Preheat oven to 200°C/400°F. Oil four holes of
a 6-hole (¾-cup/180ml) texas muffin pan.
2 Brush one sheet of pastry with butter; top with
remaining sheets, brushing each sheet with butter.
3 Using sharp knife, cut pastry into quarters. Line
pan holes with pastry; bake about 6 minutes or until
golden brown and crisp. Cool in pan.
4 Meanwhile, shell and devein prawns. Combine
prawns, lettuce, onion and half the sauce in large
bowl; season to taste.
5 Divide mixture between pastry cases; drizzle
with remaining sauce.

prep + cook time 35 minutes serves 4
nutritional count per serving 16.1g total fat
(7.4g saturated fat); 1522kJ (364 cal);
25.2g carbohydrate; 28.7g protein; 1.4g fibre

notes We used large fillo sheets measuring about
28cm x 44cm (11 inches x 17 inches) for the pastry
cups. For a healthier option, use olive-oil spray
instead of butter for pastry sheets.

School prawns can also be used, or try crab or lobster meat.

pea and broad bean frittata

¾ cup (105g) frozen broad (fava) beans
¾ cup (90g) frozen peas
6 eggs
2 tablespoons sour cream
2 tablespoons finely chopped fresh sage
1 cup (240g) ricotta cheese

1 Preheat oven to 200°C/400°F.
2 Add beans and peas to small saucepan of boiling water; return to the boil, drain. When cool enough to handle, peel broad beans.
3 Combine eggs, sour cream, sage, half the cheese and half the broad beans and peas in large bowl; season.
4 Pour egg mixture into oiled 25cm ovenproof frying pan. Cook mixture, on stove top, over medium-high heat until base is set. Transfer pan to oven. Cook frittata, uncovered, about 12 minutes or until set and browned lightly.
5 Top frittata with remaining cheese, beans and peas; place under preheated grill until cheese is melted slightly.

prep + cook time 35 minutes serves 4
nutritional count per serving 18.9g total fat (9.4g saturated fat); 1108kJ (265 cal); 3.1g carbohydrate; 19.6g protein; 2.9g fibre

serving suggestion Green salad.

fish skewers with lime, ginger and rocket

750g (1½ pounds) white fish fillets
1 tablespoon sesame oil
2 teaspoons finely grated lime rind
2 tablespoons lime juice
3 limes, extra, cut into wedges
60g (2 ounces) baby rocket leaves (arugula)
2 tablespoons thinly sliced pickled ginger
1 tablespoon ginger pickling liquid
2 tablespoons kecap manis

1 Cut fish into 2.5cm (1 inch) pieces. Combine fish, oil, rind and juice in large bowl.
2 Thread 3 pieces of fish and a lime wedge onto each skewer, season.
3 Preheat oiled grill plate (or grill or barbecue); cook skewers, in batches.
4 Combine rocket, ginger, ginger liquid and kecap manis in bowl; season to taste.
5 Serve skewers with salad.

prep + cook time 35 minutes **serves** 4
nutritional count per serving 18.1g total fat (3.3g saturated fat); 1359kJ (325 cal); 1.1g carbohydrate; 39.3g protein; 0.5g fibre

note We used swordfish steaks in this recipe, but any firm white fish fillet will be fine.

Cover the ends of the bamboo skewers in foil to prevent them from scorching during cooking. Or, if you have time, soak them in cold water for 30 minutes.

honey soy chicken with herb salad

4 x 250g (8 ounce) chicken kiev, skin on (see note)
375g (12 ounces) bottled soy, honey and
  garlic marinade
1 cup loosely packed fresh coriander leaves
  (cilantro)
1 cup loosely packed fresh mint leaves
1 cup (80g) bean sprouts
2 fresh long red chillies, sliced thinly

1 Preheat oven to 220°C/425°F.
2 Combine chicken and marinade in large bowl.
3 Heat an oiled large frying pan; cook chicken, in batches, on stove top, until browned all over. Place chicken on baking paper (parchment) lined oven tray. Transfer to oven; roast about 15 minutes or until cooked through. Cover chicken; stand 5 minutes before serving.
4 Meanwhile, combine herbs, sprouts and chilli in medium bowl. Serve chicken with herb salad.

prep + cook time 35 minutes **serves** 4
nutritional count per serving 36.4g total fat (11g saturated fat); 2508kJ (600 cal); 7.5g carbohydrate; 60.1g protein; 2.4g fibre

serving suggestion Steamed rice and lime wedges.
note The cut known as chicken kiev is a breast of chicken with the wing bone attached; this gives a small jutting-out bone on each fillet. It is available from poultry shops.

moroccan-spiced baked fish

4 whole white fish (1.2kg)
⅓ cup (60g) moroccan seasoning
125g (4 ounces) butter, softened
2 tablespoons coarsely chopped fresh herbs
100g (3 ounces) mesclun
2 medium lemons

1 Preheat oven to 220°C/425°F.
2 Score fish through the thickest part on both sides; sprinkle with seasoning. Heat oiled large frying pan; cook fish, in batches, on stove top, until skin is crisp.
3 Place fish on large baking paper (parchment) lined oven tray. Transfer to oven; cook, uncovered, about 20 minutes or until cooked through. Season.

4 Meanwhile, combine butter and herbs in small bowl; season to taste.
5 Serve fish with herb butter, mesclun and lemon cheeks.

prep + cook time 35 minutes **serves** 4
nutritional count per serving 29.5g total fat (18.2g saturated fat); 1659kJ (397 cal); 0.4g carbohydrate; 32.9g protein; 0.4g fibre

notes We used snapper in this recipe, but any whole white fish will be fine. Ask the fishmonger to clean and scale the fish for you.
Use herbs such as tarragon, chervil, lemon thyme, dill and chives.

Salmon can be marinated for 2 hours before cooking. Chicken stock can be used instead of the consommé.

barbecued salmon in brown sugar

1 cup (250ml) chicken consommé
½ cup (110g) firmly packed light brown sugar
4 salmon fillets (880g), skin on, bones removed
440g (14 ounces) hokkien noodles
45g (1½ ounces) trimmed watercress

1 Combine consommé and sugar in small saucepan; cook, stirring, until sugar dissolves. Divide mixture in half, cool. Add one portion of the cooled mixture to salmon in shallow dish; turn salmon to coat.
2 Cook salmon on heated oiled grill plate (or grill or barbecue). Cover; stand 5 minutes.
3 Meanwhile, place noodles in large heatproof bowl, cover with boiling water; separate with fork, drain.
4 Serve salmon with noodles and watercress; drizzle with remaining heated consommé. Serve with lime wedges, if you like.

prep + cook time 35 minutes serves 4
nutritional count per serving 17.1g total fat (3.9g saturated fat); 3001kJ (718 cal); 84g carbohydrate; 54.3g protein; 2.5g fibre

barbecued haloumi with tomato salad

Combine 1 finely chopped medium red onion, 250g (8 ounces) quartered cherry tomatoes, 2 tablespoons finely chopped fresh basil, ¼ cup olive oil and 2 tablespoons lemon juice in medium bowl; season to taste. Halve 360g (12 ounces) haloumi cheese lengthways then cut in half crossways. Cook haloumi on preheated grill plate (or grill or barbecue) until browned both sides. Serve haloumi with tomato mixture.

prep + cook time 35 minutes **serves** 4
nutritional count per serving 29.2g total fat (11.8g saturated fat); 1526kJ (365 cal); 5.6g carbohydrate; 20.2g protein; 1.6g fibre

note Haloumi is a firm, cream-coloured sheep's-milk cheese matured in brine; it is somewhat like a minty, salty fetta in flavour, and can be grilled or fried, briefly, without breaking down. It should be eaten while still warm as it becomes tough and rubbery on cooling.

linguine with smoked salmon and rocket

Cook 375g (12 ounces) linguine pasta in large pan of boiling water until tender; drain, return to pan. Add 75g (2½ ounces) chopped butter, 1 cup finely grated parmesan cheese, 220g (7 ounces) sliced smoked salmon, 60g (2 ounces) baby rocket leaves (arugula), 2 teaspoons finely grated lemon rind and ¼ cup lemon juice to hot pasta; toss gently, season to taste.

prep + cook time 35 minutes **serves** 4
nutritional count per serving 25.5g total fat (14.9g saturated fat); 2600kJ (622 cal); 64.7g carbohydrate; 31.4g protein; 3.4g fibre

poached eggs with lemon asparagus

Bring large saucepan of water to the boil then reduce to a simmer; stir water in a circular motion. Crack one egg into a cup; slide into the water in the centre of the pan. Add a second egg; cook 5 minutes or until the eggs are cooked to your liking. Remove with a slotted spoon, drain on absorbent paper. Cover to keep warm. Repeat with another 2 eggs. Meanwhile, cook 350g (11 ounces) asparagus on heated oiled grill plate (or grill or barbecue) about 3 minutes or until tender. Place asparagus in large bowl; add 2 tablespoons lemon juice and ¼ cup finely grated parmesan cheese; toss gently. Season to taste. Divide asparagus between serving plates; top with poached eggs, shaved parmesan and freshly ground black pepper.

prep + cook time 35 minutes **serves** 4
nutritional count per serving 7g total fat
(2.6g saturated fat); 481kJ (115 cal);
1.7g carbohydrate; 10.8g protein; 1.3g fibre

pears with palm sugar and yogurt cream

Combine ½ cup grated palm sugar, 4 torn fresh kaffir lime leaves and ¼ cup water in small saucepan; bring to the boil then simmer, uncovered, until sugar is dissolved. Remove from heat; cool. Strain syrup into jug. Meanwhile, beat ½ cup thickened (heavy) cream until soft peaks form; fold in ⅓ cup greek-style yogurt; refrigerate until required. Cut 4 small pears in half lengthways; sprinkle cut sides with 2 tablespoons caster (superfine) sugar. Cook pears, cut-side down, in heated greased medium frying pan until browned and tender. Serve pears with syrup and cream.

prep + cook time 35 minutes **serves** 4
nutritional count per serving 12.5g total fat
(8.2g saturated fat); 1158kJ (277 cal);
38.1g carbohydrate; 2.1g protein; 1.9g fibre

Serving the tarte tartin on warmed plates keeps the caramel soft.

banana tarte tatin

1 cup (220g) caster (superfine) sugar
125g (4 ounces) cold unsalted butter, chopped
1 sheet butter puff pastry
4 large bananas (520g), peeled, cut into 2cm
 (¾ inch) pieces
2 tablespoons caster (superfine) sugar, extra

1 Combine sugar with 2 tablespoons water in medium saucepan; stir over heat, without boiling, until sugar is dissolved. Bring to the boil; boil, uncovered, without stirring, about 10 minutes or until a caramel colour, remove from heat. Using a metal whisk, gradually whisk butter into caramel until combined to form a sauce. Pour sauce into 20cm (8 inch) ovenproof frying pan. Cool.
2 Meanwhile, preheat oven to 220°C/425°F.
3 Cut 23cm (9 inch) circle from pastry.

4 Place banana, cut-side up, on top of caramel; top with pastry, making sure the pastry sits evenly over the bananas. Press the overhanging pastry tightly against bananas to form an edge. Sprinkle pastry with extra sugar.
5 Bake, uncovered, about 15 minutes or until pastry is browned and cooked through. Invert onto a warmed large plate to serve.

prep + cook time 35 minutes serves 4
nutritional count per serving 35.6g total fat (17.8g saturated fat); 2989kJ (715 cal); 93.5g carbohydrate; 4g protein; 2.5g fibre

serving suggestion Ice-cream or cream.

chocolate trifle with blueberries and cream

¼ cup (55g) firmly packed light brown sugar
½ cup (125ml) sherry
2 cinnamon sticks
500g (1 pound) store-bought chocolate cake
1¼ cups (310ml) thickened (heavy) cream
 (see notes)
150g (5 ounces) fresh blueberries

1 Combine sugar, sherry and cinnamon in small saucepan; bring to the boil then simmer, uncovered, until sugar is dissolved. Cool syrup.
2 Discard any icing from cake; cut cake into 2cm (¾ inch) cubes. Divide cake between four 1½-cup (375ml) serving glasses; drizzle with syrup. Top with cream and blueberries.

prep + cook time 35 minutes **serves** 4
nutritional count per serving 51.2g total fat (32.9g saturated fat); 3557kJ (851 cal); 78.8g carbohydrate; 10.6g protein; 2.6g fibre

notes It is fine to use just 1 x 300ml carton of cream for this recipe.
Decorate trifle with chocolate shavings, if you like. Just run a sharp vegetable peeler down the side of a slightly softened block of chocolate. The harder you press the thicker the shavings will be. We used a small block of dark eating chocolate.

apple and raspberry crumbles

4 medium green apples (600g), chopped coarsely
2 teaspoons finely grated lemon rind
¼ cup (60ml) lemon juice
¼ cup (55g) firmly packed light brown sugar
2 teaspoons mixed spice
500g (1 pound) frozen raspberries
125g (4 ounces) scotch finger biscuits, crumbled

1 Preheat oven to 220°C/425°F.
2 Cook apples, rind, juice and sugar in large frying pan until apples begin to caramelise. Stir in spice, 2 tablespoons water and the raspberries.
3 Divide mixture into four 1-cup (250ml) shallow ovenproof dishes; top with biscuit crumbs. Place dishes on oven tray.
4 Bake in oven about 10 minutes or until crumbles are heated through.

prep + cook time 35 minutes **serves** 4
nutritional count per serving 8.4g total fat
(4.1g saturated fat); 1346kJ (322 cal);
53g carbohydrate; 3.9g protein; 9.5g fibre

notes We used granny smith apples in this recipe. You need 2 large lemons for the rind and juice.

serving suggestion Dust with sifted icing sugar; serve with ice-cream or double cream.

glossary

ANTIPASTO, CHAR-GRILLED marinated char-grilled vegetables, such as capsicum, eggplant, zucchini, artichoke, etc. Available from delicatessens or supermarkets.

ARTICHOKES, MARINATED the tender centre (heart) of the globe artichoke purchased canned or in glass jars in brine or oil.

ASIAN GREENS, BABY a packaged mix of baby buk choy, choy sum, gai lan and water spinach. Available from selected supermarkets.

BALSAMIC GLAZE a rich, dark brown glaze made from concentrated balsamic vinegar and brown sugar; available from major supermarkets.

BASIL an aromatic herb; there are many types, but the most commonly used is sweet, or common, basil.
thai also known as horapa; has smallish leaves and a sweet licorice/aniseed taste. Available in Asian supermarkets and greengrocers.

BEANS
borlotti also known as roman or pink beans. Interchangeable with pinto beans because of the similarity in appearance – both are pale pink or beige with dark red streaks.
broad also known as fava or windsor beans; available dried, fresh, canned and frozen. Fresh and frozen forms should be peeled twice, discarding both the outer long green pod and the beige-green tough inner shell.
four bean mix made up of kidney beans, butter beans, chickpeas and cannellini beans.
sprouts also known as bean shoots; tender new growths of assorted beans and seeds germinated for consumption as sprouts. The most readily available are mung bean, soy bean, alfalfa and snow pea sprouts.

BEEF
eye-fillet tenderloin fillet; has a fine texture and is extremely tender. Is more expensive than other cuts.
rump a tender, boneless cut taken from the upper hindquarter.
scotch fillet cut from the muscle running along the spine.

BEETROOT also known as red beets or beets; firm, round root vegetable.

BISCUITS
scotch finger made from flour, sugar, butter, egg and condensed milk; can be broken into two finger-sized pieces.
sponge finger also known as savoy biscuits, savoiardi or lady's fingers; these Italian-style crisp fingers are made from sponge-cake mixture.

BREAD
brioche rich, yeast-risen French bread made with butter and eggs. Available from pâtisseries and better bakeries.
ciabatta in Italian it means 'slipper,' which is the traditional shape of this popular white bread with a crisp crust.
tortillas thin, round unleavened bread originating in Mexico; two kinds are available, one made from wheat flour and the other from corn (maize meal).

BREADCRUMBS, STALE one- or two-day-old bread made into crumbs by blending or processing.

BUTTER use salted or unsalted butter; 125g is equal to one stick (4 ounces).

BUTTERMILK originally the term given to the slightly sour liquid left after butter was churned from cream, today it is made similarly to yogurt. Sold alongside all fresh milk products in supermarkets; despite the implication of its name, it's low in fat.

CAJUN SPICE MIX a blend of herbs and spices including basil, paprika, tarragon, onion, fennel, thyme and cayenne; available at spice shops and most supermarkets.

CAPERS the grey-green buds of a warm climate shrub, sold either dried and salted or pickled in a vinegar brine. *Baby capers*, those picked early, are very small, fuller-flavoured and more expensive than the full-sized ones. Capers, whether packed in brine or in salt, must be rinsed well before using.

CHEESE
bocconcini walnut-sized, fresh, baby mozzarella, a delicate, semi-soft, white cheese. Spoils rapidly, so must be kept under refrigeration, in brine, for one or two days at most.

cheddar this semi-hard cows'-milk cheese is eaten throughout the world.
fetta a crumbly goat- or sheep-milk cheese with a sharp salty taste.
goat's made from goats' milk; has an earthy, strong taste. Comes in soft and firm textures and in various shapes and sizes; may be rolled in ash or herbs.
mascarpone fresh, unripened, smooth, triple cream cheese with a rich, sweet, slightly acidic, taste.
parmesan also known as parmigiana; a hard, grainy cows'-milk cheese.
ricotta a sweet, moist, low-fat, fresh unripened cheese made from whey.

CHERVIL also known as cicily; a curly-leafed herb with a mild fennel flavour.

CHICKEN
tenderloin thin strip of meat lying just under the breast.
thigh fillet thigh with the skin and centre bone removed.

CHILLI available in many different types and sizes. Use rubber gloves when seeding and chopping fresh chillies as they can burn your skin. Removing seeds and membranes lessens the heat level.
flakes deep-red, dehydrated chilli slices and whole seeds.
jam a sweet, sourish tangy jam sold in jars at supermarkets or Asian food stores. Used in sauces, stir-fries and some soups. After opening, store in the refrigerator.
long red available fresh and dried; a generic term used for any moderately hot, long (6cm-8cm), thin chilli.
red thai small, medium hot and bright red in colour.

CHOCOLATE, DARK EATING also known as semi-sweet or luxury chocolate; made of a high percentage of cocoa liquor and cocoa butter, and a little added sugar.

CHORIZO a sausage of Spanish origin. Is made of coarsely ground pork and is highly seasoned with garlic and chillies.

CINNAMON dried inner bark of the shoots of the cinnamon tree; available in stick (quill) or ground form.

CONSOMMÉ a clear soup usually of beef, veal or chicken.

CORIANDER also known as pak chee, cilantro or chinese parsley; bright-green leafy herb with a pungent flavour. Both the stems and roots are used, so wash well before using. Also available ground or as seeds; these should not be substituted for fresh coriander as the tastes are completely different.

COUSCOUS a fine, grain-like cereal product made from a semolina dough, sieved then dehydrated to produce tiny even-sized pellets of couscous; it is rehydrated by steaming, or with the addition of a warm liquid, and swells to three or four times its original size.

CRANBERRIES, DRIED have the same slightly sour, succulent flavour as fresh cranberries. Available in health-food stores and most supermarkets.

CREAM we use fresh cream, also known as pure cream and pouring cream, unless otherwise stated.
sour a thick, cultured soured cream.
thickened a whipping cream.

CUCUMBER
lebanese short, slender and thin-skinned. Probably the most popular variety because of its tender, edible skin, tiny, yielding seeds, and sweet, fresh taste.
telegraph also known as the european or burpless cucumber; long (35cm and more) and slender, its thin dark-green skin has shallow ridges running down its length.

CURRY PASTES recipes in this book call for commercially prepared pastes of varying strengths and flavours. Use whichever one you feel suits your spice-level tolerance best.
green the hottest of the traditional Thai pastes; particularly good in chicken curries.
laksa generally medium in heat, laksa curry always contains coconut milk and rice stick noodles; goes best with seafood, tofu, vegetables and chicken.
tandoori a mild blend of tomato, ginger, garlic, paprika, lemon juice, onion and various spices blended with yogurt and used as a marinade.

CURRY POWDER a blend of ground spices, including dried chilli, cumin, cinnamon, coriander, fennel, mace, fenugreek, cardamom and turmeric. Can be mild or hot.

FENNEL also known as finocchio or anise; a pale green/white, firm, crisp, roundish vegetable about 8cm-12cm in diameter. The bulb has a slightly sweet, anise flavour, but the leaves have a much stronger taste. Also the name given to the dried seeds having a licorice flavour.

FISH FILLETS, FIRM WHITE blue eye, bream, flathead, swordfish, whiting, ling, jewfish, snapper or sea perch are all good choices. Check for any small pieces of bone in the fillets and use tweezers to remove them.

FLOUR, SELF-RAISING plain (all-purpose) flour sifted with baking powder in the proportion of 1 cup flour to 2 teaspoons baking powder.

GAI LAN also known as chinese broccoli, gai larn, kanah, gai lum and chinese kale; appreciated more for its stems than its coarse leaves.

GINGER also known as green or root ginger; the thick root of a tropical plant. *Pickled ginger* is sold in pieces or sliced, and comes in red and pink varieties packed in a seasoned brine.

GNOCCHI is the Italian name for a variety of dumpling. They may be made from potato, semolina, ordinary wheat flour, bread crumbs or a number of other ingredients, such as polenta.

HARISSA a Moroccan paste or sauce made from dried chillies, cumin, garlic, oil and caraway seeds. The paste, available in a tube, is very hot and should not be used in large amounts; bottled harissa sauce has less heat. Available from Middle-Eastern grocery stores and some supermarkets.

HUMMUS a Middle-Eastern salad or dip made from softened dried chickpeas, garlic, lemon juice and tahini (sesame seed paste); can be purchased, ready-made, from most delicatessens and supermarkets.

KAFFIR LIME LEAVES also known as bai magrood; the aromatic leaves of a citrus tree. Looks like two glossy dark green leaves joined end to end, forming a rounded hourglass shape. Used fresh or dried similarly to bay or curry leaves. A strip of fresh lime peel may be substituted for each kaffir lime leaf.

KUMARA the Polynesian name of an orange-fleshed sweet potato that is often confused with yam.

LAMB
backstrap (fillet) the larger fillet from a row of loin chops or cutlets.
cutlets small, tender rib chops.

LEMON GRASS a tall, clumping, lemon-smelling and -tasting, sharp-edged grass; the white lower part of the stem is chopped and used in Asian cooking.

LEMON PEPPER SEASONING a blend of crushed black pepper, lemon, herbs and spices. Available in most supermarkets.

MESCLUN a salad mix of assorted young lettuce and other green leaves, including baby spinach leaves, mizuna and curly endive.

MIRIN a champagne-coloured Japanese cooking wine; made of glutinous rice and alcohol and used expressly for cooking. Should not be confused with sake.

MISO Japan's famous bean paste made from fermented soya beans and rice, rye or barley. It varies in colour, texture and saltiness. It is a common ingredient in soups, sauces and dressings. Available from Asian food stores and major supermarkets.

MIXED SALAD LEAVES also sold as mixed baby leaves, salad mix, mesclun or gourmet salad mix; a mixture of assorted young lettuce and other green leaves.

MOROCCAN SEASONING available from most Middle-Eastern food stores, spice shops and major supermarkets. Turmeric, cinnamon and cumin add an authentic Moroccan flavouring to dishes.

MUSTARD SEED OIL rich and full-bodied with a buttery, nutty flavour, but without the heat or strong mustard taste. Cold-pressed oil is pressed from the whole seed, with no heat treatment, and is then filtered and bottled. It has a low saturated fat content and is high in omega-3 and monounsaturated fats.

NOODLES

bean thread (wun sen) also known as cellophane or glass noodles because they are transparent when cooked. Made from mung bean paste; white in colour (not off-white like rice vermicelli), very delicate and fine. Available dried in various-sized bundles; soak to soften before using.

hokkien also known as stir-fry noodles; fresh wheat noodles resembling thick, yellow-brown spaghetti needing no pre-cooking before being used.

rice vermicelli also known as sen mee, mei fun or bee hoon; similar to bean threads, only longer and are made with rice flour instead of mung bean starch.

PAPRIKA a ground, dried, sweet red capsicum (bell pepper); there are many types available, including sweet, hot, mild and smoked.

POTATOES

baby new also known as chats; not a separate variety, but an early harvest with very thin skin; good unpeeled.

desiree oval, smooth and pink-skinned with a waxy yellow flesh. Good in salads, boiled and roasted.

RICE

basmati a white, fragrant long-grained rice. It should be washed several times before cooking.

jasmine fragrant long-grained rice; white rice can be substituted, but will not taste the same.

long-grain elongated grain, remains separate when cooked; most popular steaming rice in Asia.

pre-cooked is milled, completely cooked then dried. In its dried form, pre-cooked rice has a more porous and open appearance so that the boiling water can penetrate the grain and rehydrate it in a short time.

SAUCES

barbecue a spicy, tomato-based sauce used to baste or as a condiment.

cranberry made from cranberries cooked in a sugar syrup.

fish also called nam pla or nuoc nam; made from pulverised salted fermented fish, most often anchovies. Has a pungent smell and strong taste, so use sparingly.

hoisin a thick, sweet and spicy Chinese paste made from salted fermented soya beans, onions and garlic.

soy made from fermented soya beans. Several variations are available in most supermarkets and Asian food stores. We use a mild Japanese variety in our recipes unless stated otherwise; possibly the best table soy and the one to choose if you only want one variety.

kecap manis a dark, thick, sweet soy sauce. The soy's sweetness is derived from the addition of either molasses or palm sugar when brewed.

light soy a thin, pale, salty-tasting sauce; used in dishes in which the natural colour is to be maintained. Not to be confused with salt-reduced or low-sodium soy sauces.

sweet chilli a mild, Thai-style sauce made from red chillies, sugar, garlic and vinegar.

tomato also known as ketchup or catsup; made from tomatoes, vinegar and spices.

tomato pasta made from a blend of tomatoes, herbs and spices.

SILVER BEET also known as swiss chard or blettes; may mistakenly be called spinach. A member of the beet family grown for its tasty green leaves and celery-like stems.

SUGAR

brown extremely soft, finely granulated sugar retaining molasses for its colour and flavour. *Dark brown* is moist, with a distinctive rich, full flavour coming from natural molasses.

caster also known as superfine or finely granulated table sugar.

icing also known as confectioners' or powdered sugar; granulated sugar crushed together with a small amount of cornflour.

palm also known as nam tan pip, jawa, jaggery or gula melaka; made from the sap of the sugar palm tree. Light brown to black in colour and usually sold in rock-hard cakes. Substitute it with brown sugar if unavailable.

white a coarsely granulated table sugar, also known as crystal sugar.

SULTANAS dried grapes, also known as golden raisins.

SUMAC a purple-red, astringent spice ground from berries growing on shrubs that flourish wild around the Mediterranean; adds a tart, lemony flavour to food. Available from Middle-Eastern food stores and major supermarkets.

TAHINI sesame seed paste.

VEAL

cutlets choice chop from the mid-loin (back) area.

schnitzel thinly sliced steak available crumbed or plain; we used plain (uncrumbed) schnitzel in our recipes.

VINEGAR

balsamic originally from Modena, Italy, there are now many balsamic vinegars on the market; is a deep rich brown colour with a sweet and sour flavour. *balsamic white vinegar* (condiment) is a clear, lighter version of balsamic vinegar; has a fresh, sweet, clean taste.

cider (apple cider) made from fermented apples.

red wine based on fermented red wine.

white wine made from a blend of white wines.

WATERCRESS also known as winter rocket. Is one of the cress family, a large group of peppery greens. Highly perishable, so must be used as soon as possible after purchase.

WITLOF (belgian endive) cigar-shaped, tightly packed heads with pale, yellow-green tips. Has a delicately bitter flavour. May be cooked or eaten raw.

ZUCCHINI also known as courgette; small, pale- or dark-green, yellow or white vegetable belonging to the squash family. Harvested when young, its edible flowers can be stuffed then deep-fried or oven-baked.

conversion chart

MEASURES

One Australian metric measuring cup holds approximately 250ml; one Australian metric tablespoon holds 20ml; one Australian metric teaspoon holds 5ml.

The difference between one country's measuring cups and another's is within a two- or three-teaspoon variance, and will not affect your cooking results. North America, New Zealand and the United Kingdom use a 15ml tablespoon.

All cup and spoon measurements are level. The most accurate way of measuring dry ingredients is to weigh them. When measuring liquids, use a clear glass or plastic jug with either metric or imperial markings.

We use large eggs with an average weight of 60g.

OVEN TEMPERATURES

The oven temperatures in this book are for conventional ovens; if you have a fan-forced oven, decrease the temperature by 10-20 degrees.

	°C (CELSIUS)	°F (FAHRENHEIT)
Very slow	120	250
Slow	150	300
Moderately slow	160	325
Moderate	180	350
Moderately hot	200	400
Hot	220	425
Very hot	240	475

DRY MEASURES

METRIC	IMPERIAL
15g	½oz
30g	1oz
60g	2oz
90g	3oz
125g	4oz (¼lb)
155g	5oz
185g	6oz
220g	7oz
250g	8oz (½lb)
280g	9oz
315g	10oz
345g	11oz
375g	12oz (¾lb)
410g	13oz
440g	14oz
470g	15oz
500g	16oz (1lb)
750g	24oz (1½lb)
1kg	32oz (2lb)

LIQUID MEASURES

METRIC	IMPERIAL
30ml	1 fluid oz
60ml	2 fluid oz
100ml	3 fluid oz
125ml	4 fluid oz
150ml	5 fluid oz
190ml	6 fluid oz
250ml	8 fluid oz
300ml	10 fluid oz
500ml	16 fluid oz
600ml	20 fluid oz
1000ml (1 litre)	1¾ pints

LENGTH MEASURES

METRIC	IMPERIAL
3mm	⅛in
6mm	¼in
1cm	½in
2cm	¾in
2.5cm	1in
5cm	2in
6cm	2½in
8cm	3in
10cm	4in
13cm	5in
15cm	6in
18cm	7in
20cm	8in
23cm	9in
25cm	10in
28cm	11in
30cm	12in (1ft)

index

First Published in 2010 by ACP Magazines Ltd,
a division of PBL Media Pty Limited
54 Park St, Sydney
GPO Box 4088, Sydney, NSW 2001.
phone (02) 9282 8618; fax (02) 9267 9438
acpbooks@acpmagazines.com.au; www.acpbooks.com.au

ACP BOOKS
General Manager - Christine Whiston
Editor-in-Chief - Susan Tomnay
Creative Director & Designer - Hieu Chi Nguyen
Food Director - Pamela Clark

Published and Distributed in the United Kingdom by Octopus Publishing Group
Endeavour House
189 Shaftesbury Avenue
London WC2H 8JY
United Kingdom
phone (+44)(0)207 632 5400; fax (+44)(0)207 632 5405
info@octopus-publishing.co.uk;
www.octopusbooks.co.uk

Printed by Toppan Printing Co., China

International foreign language rights, Brian Cearnes, ACP Books bcearnes@acpmagazines.com.au

A catalogue record for this book is available from the British Library.
ISBN 978-1-86396-942-0

© ACP Magazines Ltd 2010
ABN 18 053 273 546